Jerzy Robert Wilk

ENGLISH IRREGULAR VERBS

ENGLISH IRREGULAR VERBS

300 ENGLISH IRREGULAR VERBS

LEVEL A1-C2

Jerzy Robert Wilk

Author: *Jerzy Robert Wilk*

Proofreading: *Alex Bradshaw*

Graphic design for cover: *Jerzy Robert Wilk*

First published 2021

ISBN: 978-83-67269-00-1

ISBN: 978-83-67269-02-5

Edition 1

Cardiff 2022

CONTENTS

INTRODUCTION

This textbook has been written for people learning English at different levels and who want to consolidate or supplement their knowledge of irregular verb forms. In fact, English regular verbs generally do not pose much of a problem to learners as long as they know the basic rules about how they function and how to form past simple and past participle forms.

Irregular verb forms, however, must be learnt by heart, as they have their own rules. Remember that both regular and irregular verbs in the present simple tense follow the same conjugation rules (except for the verbs *be* and *have*).

Sadly, there is no rule to help distinguish regular verbs from irregular verbs. However, if you memorise the list of irregular verbs at the end of the book, you can safely assume that any verb not on the list belongs is regular, not least because they make up the vast majority of verbs.

The 300 English irregular verbs discussed in this book are divided into three groups. The first contains those irregular verbs where the infinitive form, the past simple form and the past participle form are different, as well as those irregular verbs where the past tense form or the past participle form is the same as the infinitive. The second group contains irregular verbs where the past simple and the past participle forms are the same, and the third group contains irregular verbs where the infinitive, past simple and past participle forms are identical in spelling, though in a few cases they do differ in pronunciation.

Each irregular verb is presented in three forms: infinitive, past simple and past participle. Underneath the infinitive form you will find its synonyms. Inside slash marks // a British phonetic transcription is given to facilitate the correct pronunciation of the verb forms.

Some verbs in British English are irregular, while in American English they are regular, and sometimes vice versa. For this reason, if an irregular verb in British English has an American form, this form is included, with a icon next to it. This means that the form is mainly used by speakers of American English.

If there is a icon next to the verb, it means the verb form is mainly used by speakers of British English. If there are no icons next to the verb, it means that the verb is used commonly in both British and American English.

The use of each irregular verb and its forms is illustrated by several example sentences, making it much easier to remember the forms in context.

The topic on irregular verbs presented in the book will help to enrich and expand both the practical and correct use of them. Chapter 7 (page 113) contains a number of tests to check your knowledge of irregular verb forms after studying them.

Happy reading!

Author

THE INTERNATIONAL PHONETIC ALPHABET (IPA)

The International Phonetic Alphabet is a standardised phonetic transcription system containing a set of symbols that linguists use to describe sounds in spoken language. Below is a simplified table of these symbols that are helpful to learners of English.

SINGLE VOWELS

ɪ	i:	ʊ	u:
ship /ʃɪp/	**see** /si:/	**book** /bʊk/	**food** /fu:d/
e	ɜ:	ə	ɔ:
bed /bed/	**bird** /bɜ:d/	**about** /əˈbaʊt/	**ball** /bɔ:l/
æ	ʌ	ɒ	ɑ:
cat /kæt/	**cup** /kʌp/	**hot** /hɒt/	**car** /kɑ:(r)/

DIPHTHONGS

eɪ	ɔɪ	aɪ	əʊ
make /meɪk/	**coin** /kɔɪn/	**rice** /raɪs/	**go** /gəʊ/
eə	ɪə	ʊə	aʊ
bear /beə(r)/	**here** /hɪə(r)/	**moor** /mʊə(r)/	**brown** /braʊn/

UNVOICED CONSONANTS

p	f	θ	t	s	ʃ	ʧ	k
pea /pi:/	**fox** /fɒks/	**teeth** /ti:θ/	**tree** /tri:/	**soap** /səʊp/	**show** /ʃəʊ/	**cheese** /tʃi:z/	**cook** /kʊk/

VOICED CONSONANTS

b	v	ð	d	z	ʒ	ʤ	g
bag /bæg/	**vet** /vet/	**that** /ðæt/	**dog** /dɒg/	**zoo** /zu:/	**vision** /ˈvɪʒn/	**jazz** /dʒæz/	**green** /gri:n/
m	n	ŋ	h	w	l	r	j
mask /ˈmɑ:sk/	**night** /naɪt/	**thing** /θɪŋ/	**ham** /hæm/	**we** /wi/	**leap** /li:p/	**red** /red/	**you** /ju/

1. IN BRIEF

1.1. WHAT IS A VERB?

A verb is a part of speech that expresses an action or a state. The basic form of a verb is *the infinitive*. In many languages a verb can be easily distinguished from other parts of speech, such as nouns or adjectives, by characteristic endings. For example, in Polish, the infinitive form of a verb usually ends in -ć or, more rarely, in -c. In French, regular verbs have -er and -ir ending in the infinitive, and in Spanish, most regular verbs end in -ar, -er, or -ir in the infinitive.

In English, however, verbs in the infinitive do not have homogeneous endings and vary greatly, e.g., *drive, walk, run, paint, go, kiss*. Look at the table below to compare English infinitives with those from other languages.

English infinitive	Polish infinitive	Spanish infinitive	French infinitive	Italian infinitive
like	*lubi**ć***	*gust**ar***	*aim**er***	*piace**re***
cook	*gotowa**ć***	*cocin**ar***	*prépar**er***	*cuoce**re***
eat	*jeś**ć***	*com**er***	*mang**er***	*mangia**re***
scream	*krzycze**ć***	*grit**ar***	*cri**er***	*grida**re***
clean	*sprząta**ć***	*limpi**ar***	*nettoy**er***	*puli**re***
write	*pisa**ć***	*escrib**ir***	*écri**re***	*scrive**re***
hide	*ukrywa**ć***	*escond**er***	*cach**er***	*nasconde**re***
feel	*czu**ć***	*sent**ir***	*sent**ir***	*senti**re***

1.2. CLASSIFICATION OF VERBS

In English, two very important groups of verbs are action verbs – those that express some kind of movement, describe what happens to something or someone, or what someone or something does – and state verbs. The most commonly used state verbs are: *be, have, like, hate, prefer, want, need.*

Other verbs expressing state are:

1. Verbs expressing senses such as: *feel, see, hear, smell, taste.*
2. Verbs of thinking such as: *think, understand, know, believe, remember.*
3. Other state verbs: *cost, own, agree, wish.*

The above division into action verbs and state verbs is important because some English verbs can be both action verbs and state verbs at the same time, so you have to remember to use the correct grammatical tense with them.

For example, the verb *have* as a state verb means "to possess", so in this case the verb *have* cannot be used with continuous tenses such as the present continuous or the past continuous.

However, *have* can also be used as an action verb, meaning "to eat", or "to drink". In this case, it can be used in the continuous tense, for example: I'm *having* lunch now.

The table below contains other English verbs that can be either an action verb or a state verb, depending on how you want to use them.

verb	action meaning	state meaning
be	*behave, act (differently than usually)*	*exist*
expect	*await sb/sth*[1]	*assume*
feel	*touch sth*	*be in a specific emotional state*
have	*drink, eat*	*possess, own*
look	*direct your eyes at sb/sth*	*have an appearance*
measure	*check how many metres/kilometres sth has by measuring it*	*have a certain length/width*
see	*meet, visit, watch*	*understand, see with your eyes*
smell	*check how sth smells*	*have a certain smell*
taste	*check the flavour of sth*	*have a certain flavour*
think	*consider*	*have an opinion*
weigh	*check how many kilograms sth has by weighing it*	*have a certain weight*

English verbs can be divided into several different categories. Among these are:

- modal verbs
- auxiliary verbs
- state and action verbs (*see above*)
- transitive and intransitive verbs

[1] *sb=somebody/sth=something*

- regular and irregular verbs

Relevant to this textbook is the classification of verbs into regular verbs and irregular verbs.

QUIZ 1

1. Action verbs are verbs that express:

a) movement
b) state

2. Action verbs cannot be used with the present simple tense.

a) true
b) false

3. The basic form of the verb is:

a) past participle
b) past simple
c) infinitive

4. The verb *see* in the sense of "*to meet*" is:

a) a state verb
b) an action verb

5. In the sentence *I think he is irresponsible*, the verb *think* is:

a) a state verb
b) both an action and a state verb
c) an action verb

6. All English verbs in the infinitive have homogenous endings.

a) true
b) false

7. Which of the following sentences is correct?

a) She's being very helpful today.
b) This salad is tasting delicious.
c) She's measuring the window to fit the nets.

2. REGULAR VERBS

2.1. FORMS OF REGULAR VERBS

Regular verbs come in five basic forms. These are:

1. infinitive
2. third person singular present simple
3. past simple, used to express the past aspect
4. past participle, used to form the passive voice and perfect tenses
5. present participle, a verb with the characteristic *-ing* ending

infinitive	3rd person singular present tense	simple past	past participle	present participle
work	*works*	*worked*	*worked*	*working*
cry	*cries*	*cried*	*cried*	*crying*
smile	*smiles*	*smiled*	*smiled*	*smiling*
play	*plays*	*played*	*played*	*playing*
call	*calls*	*called*	*called*	*calling*
cook	*cooks*	*cooked*	*cooked*	*cooking*

Most English verbs are regular verbs and subject to conjugation, which is the same for all regular verbs. The changes that occur when these verbs are conjugated to express the present simple, the past simple and the third form of the verb, the past participle, are as follows:

2.2. THE PRESENT SIMPLE TENSE

The present simple is the present tense used to express general and universal truths, habits and customs, regular actions that are repeated at certain intervals (either general, e.g. *often, sometimes, rarely, never, from time to time, occasionally*, etc, or specific, e.g. *on Fridays*) and instructions. The present simple tense is formed by adding **-es**/**-s** to a verb in the third person singular in affirmative sentences, the auxiliary **don't/doesn't** + *infinitive* in negative sentences, and **do/does** in interrogative sentences. For example:

- She **wakes** up at 6 am every day.
- She **doesn't wake** up at 6 am every day.
- **Does** she **wake** up at 6 am every day?

In the present simple, the regular verb is only changed in the third person singular by adding **-s**, or less often, **-es**, to the base form of the verb. In the other persons (e.g. first person singular), the verb does not change and has the same form as the infinitive. For example:

singular	1st person	I	*work*	*play*	*cry*	*kiss*	*love*
	2nd person	you	*work*	*play*	*cry*	*kiss*	*love*
	3rd person	he	*works*	*plays*	*cries*	*kisses*	*loves*
		she	*works*	*plays*	*cries*	*kisses*	*loves*
		it	*works*	*plays*	*cries*	*kisses*	*loves*
plural	1st person	we	*work*	*play*	*cry*	*kiss*	*love*
	2nd person	you	*work*	*play*	*cry*	*kiss*	*love*
	3rd person	they	*work*	*play*	*cry*	*kiss*	*love*

As mentioned, most regular verbs only add the ending **-s** to the third person singular (*he, she, it*) in the present simple tense. For some verbs, however, it is necessary to add the ending **-es**, and for some it is also necessary to change the spelling. The rules are:

a) Add **-s** to most regular verbs in the third person singular (*he, she, it*), e.g.

- she works
- he plays
- it talks

b) If the infinitive form ends in *-ss, -ch, sh, -x, -o*, add **-es** in the third person singular (*he, she, it*), e.g.

- she kisses
- it goes
- he fixes

c) If the infinitive form ends in *a consonant* + *y*, then we drop the *y* and add **-ies** in the third person singular (*he, she, it*), e.g.

- cry – she cries
- study – he studies
- carry – she carries

d) If the verb ends in *a vowel* + *y*, only **-s** is added for *he, she, it*, e.g.

- play – he plays
- buy – she buys
- annoy – it annoys

e) The verbs ‘*be*’ and ‘*have*’ have irregular forms in the present simple tense:

- He is, she is, it is or he’s, she’s, it’s
- He has (got), she has (got), it has (got) or he’s got, she’s got, it’s got.

f) Modal verbs have the same form for all persons, both singular and plural, e.g.

- I can, you can, she can, he can, we can, they can.

QUIZ 2

1. The past simple verb form expresses an action in the:

a) future
b) past
c) present

2. The present simple verb form expresses an action in the:

a) future
b) present
c) past

3. In the present simple tense, a regular verb is subject to change in the:

a) third person singular
b) third person singular and plural
c) third person plural

4. In the present simple tense, verbs in the singular infinitive for *he, she, it* end in:

a) -ed/-es
b) -se/-s
c) -s/-es

5. **Which of the following verb forms in the present simple tense is correct?**

    a) she kisses
    b) he cryes
    c) she kiss
    d) he fixes

6. **If an infinitive ends in *a vowel* + *y*, the third person singular of the simple present tense will add the ending:**

    a) -s
    b) -es

7. **If an infinitive ends in *a consonant* + *y*, in the third person singular of the present simple we:**

    a) cut off the 'y' and add *-ies* to the verb
    b) cut off the 'y' and add *-es* to the verb
    c) replace the ending 'y' with *-s* or *-es*

2.3. PRONUNCIATION OF FINAL 'S'

Before you learn the simple rules about how to correctly pronounce the -**s** ending in English, you need to know what a voiced consonant, a voiceless consonant and a sibilant consonant are.

- **Voiced consonant**

A voiced consonant is a consonant that produces a vibration in the vocal cords when it is pronounced.

- **Voiceless consonant**

A voiceless consonant is a consonant that doesn't produce any vibration in the vocal cords when it is pronounced.

- **Sibilant consonant**

A sibilant consonant is a consonant which produces a hissing sound similar to the hiss of a snake (ssssss) or a tone similar to zzzzzz and shhhhh (as in the words *kiss, bus, wish*) when pronounced.

To check whether a consonant is voiced or unvoiced, put a finger against your larynx while pronouncing it. If you feel your vocal cords vibrate, it means the consonant is voiced; if there is no vibration, the consonant is voiceless.

The following rules for the pronunciation of -s at the end of a word apply to verbs in the third person singular (*he, she, it*), plural nouns and the Saxon Genitive (*possessive 's*). The rules are:

a) If a verb (word) ends in a voiceless consonant, -**s** is pronounced as /s/, e.g.

- he sleep**s** /sli:ps/
- she work**s** /wɜ:ks/
- I have two cup**s** /kʌps/
- Whose book**s** /bʊks/ are they?

b) If a verb (word) ends in a voiced consonant -**s** is pronounced as /z/, e.g.

- it goe**s** /gəʊz/
- she smile**s** /smaɪlz/
- I bought two pen**s** /penz/

c) If a verb or other word ends in a sibilant consonant (hissing sound – c, s, x, z, ss, ch, sh, ge), then -**s** is pronounced as /ɪz/, e.g.

- she kiss**es** /kɪsɪz/
- it fix**es** /fɪksɪz/
- the bus**es** left /bʌsɪz/

QUIZ 3

1. A voiced consonant is a consonant that does not produce vibrations in the vocal cords when it is pronounced.

a) true
b) false

2. **Which of the following are voiced consonants?**

    a) w, z, y
    b) p, t, f
    c) d, g, m

3. **In which of the following words is there a sibilant consonant ('hissing' consonant)?**

    a) wishes
    b) gloves
    c) buses

4. **In the words *prizes, garages, changes* and *sandwiches* the final 's' is pronounced as:**

    a) /z/
    b) /ɪz/
    c) /s/

5. **In the words *students, writes* and *months* the final 's' is pronounced as:**

    a) /s/
    b) /z/
    c) /ɪz/

6. **In the words *dreams, plays* and *clothes* the final 's' is pronounced as:**

    a) /ɪz/
    b) /s/
    c) /z/

2.4. THE PAST SIMPLE TENSE

The past simple is a past tense that expresses actions and states that are completely finished in the past. Past Simple is used to express past actions and states, telling you when they happened at a more or less specific time in the past. It is used with the following time expressions: *in 2007, in 1981*, etc., *last week, last year, 10 years ago, yesterday, the other day, a long time ago, when I was a child, as a teenager,* etc.

In affirmative sentences, -ed/-d is added to the main verb in all persons singular and plural (if the main verb is a regular verb). In negative sentences the auxiliary **did not (didn't)** + *infinitive* is used, and **did** in interrogative sentences, e.g.

- I **called** you yesterday.
- I **didn't call** you yesterday.
- **Did** you **call** me yesterday?

To express the past using the past simple tense, i.e. an action that took place in the past, the ending -**ed**, or less commonly, -**d**, is added to the base verb in all singulars and plurals. This rule only applies to affirmative sentences, as in question and negative sentences the regular verb returns to its original infinitive form, e.g.

	work	***play***	***cry***	***kiss***	***love***	***stop***
I	*work**ed***	*play**ed***	*cr**ied***	*kiss**ed***	*love**d***	*stop**ped***
you	*work**ed***	*play**ed***	*cr**ied***	*kiss**ed***	*love**d***	*stop**ped***
he	*work**ed***	*play**ed***	*cr**ied***	*kiss**ed***	*love**d***	*stop**ped***
she	*work**ed***	*play**ed***	*cr**ied***	*kiss**ed***	*love**d***	*stop**ped***
it	*work**ed***	*play**ed***	*cr**ied***	*kiss**ed***	*love**d***	*stop**ped***
we	*work**ed***	*play**ed***	*cr**ied***	*kiss**ed***	*love**d***	*stop**ped***
you	*work**ed***	*play**ed***	*cr**ied***	*kiss**ed***	*love**d***	*stop**ped***
they	*work**ed***	*play**ed***	*cr**ied***	*kiss**ed***	*love**d***	*stop**ped***

As you can see in the table above, with some verbs the ending **-ed** has been added, with others **-d** has been added, and with some spelling changes have been made before adding **-ed**. The rules are:

a) For most regular verbs, **-ed** is added to the infinitive in all persons singular and plural to form the past simple tense, e.g.

- talk + **ed** = talk**ed**
- walk + **ed** = walk**ed**
- look + **ed** = look**ed**

b) If a regular verb ends in an *-e* that is not pronounced, then only **-d** is added, e.g.

- smil*e* + **d** = smile**d**

- arriv*e* + **d** = arrive**d**
- lov*e* + **d** = love**d**

c) If a regular verb ends in *a consonant + y* in the infinitive, then we replace the *y* with an *i* and add **-ed**, e.g.

- cr*y* + **ed** = cr**ied**
- stud*y* + **ed** = stud**ied**
- appl*y* + **ed** = appl**ied**

d) If a regular verb ends in *a vowel + y* in the infinitive, then **-ed** is added, e.g.

- pl*ay* + **ed** = play**ed**
- enj*oy* + **ed** = enjoy**ed**
- ob*ey* + **ed** = obey**ed**

e) If a verb ends in *a consonant + vowel + consonant*, then we double the last consonant and add **-ed**, e.g.

- *stop* + **ed** = stop**ped**
- ad*mit* + **ed** + admit**ted**
- p*lan* + **ed** = plan**ned**

f) If a verb has two syllables, ends in *a vowel + consonant + vowel*, and the stress is on the first syllable, then the last vowel is not doubled before adding **-ed**, e.g.

- o*ffer* + **ed** = offer**ed**
- en*ter* + **ed** = enter**ed**

g) If the last syllable of a verb is not stressed, or the verb ends in -w, -x, -y, then the last vowel is not doubled, e.g.

- enjoy + **ed** = enjoy**ed**
- fix + **ed** = fix**ed**
- snow + **ed** = snow**ed**

h) If a verb ends in *c*, we add **k** and then the ending **-ed**, e.g.

- mimic + **k** + **ed** = mimic**ked**
- panic + **k** + **ed** = panic**ked**
- frolic + **k** + **ed** = frolic**ked**

i) If a verb in the infinitive ends in *a vowel* + *consonant* + *l*, then the final *l* is doubled, e.g.

- trav*el* + **l** + **ed** = travel**led**
- canc*el* + **l** + **ed** = cancel**led**
- fu*el* + **l** + **ed** = fuel**led**

This rule only applies to British English, as in American English the *l* is not doubled. Compare:

- trave*ll*ed, cance*ll*ed, fue*ll*ed, mode*ll*ed, counse*ll*ed – *British English*
- trave*l*ed, cance*l*ed, fue*l*ed, mode*l*ed, counse*l*ed – *American English*

EXCEPTIONS

a) In verbs where the stress falls on the second syllable the final *l* is doubled in both British and American English, e.g.

- expel – expe*ll*ed
- control – contro*ll*ed
- patrol – patro*ll*ed
- extol – exto*ll*ed

b) In the verb *appeal*, the final *l* is not doubled, e.g.

- appeal – appealed

c) In British English, the final *l* is doubled in the verb *enrol* and *fulfil*, while in American English the verbs *enroll* and *fulfill* already end in a double *l* in the infinitive, so the third *l* is not added, e.g.

- enrol – enrolled
- fulfil – fulfilled
- enroll – enrolled
- fulfill – fulfilled

QUIZ 4

1. The simple past is a past tense that is formed by adding which ending to a regular verb in affirmative sentences?

a) *-es* or *-es*
b) *-ed* or *-d*
c) none

2. In past simple affirmative sentences, regular verbs take the ending -*ed* or -*d*:

a) in all singular and plural persons
b) only in the third person singular
c) only in the third person plural

3. In the past simple tense in negative and interrogative sentences the verb form is:

a) past participle
b) past simple
c) infinitive

4. If a regular verb ends in -*e*, then in the past simple tense we:

a) Add *-d* to it
b) Add *-ed* to it
c) Omit the *-e* and add *-d* to it

5. Which of the following statements about the past simple tense is correct?

a) If a regular verb ends in *a consonant + vowel + consonant*, then we add *-d* to it.
b) If a regular verb ends in *a consonant + y* in the infinitive, then we replace the *y* with an *i* and add *-ed.*
c) If a regular verb ends in *a vowel + y* in the infinitive, then we add *-ed* to it.
d) If a verb ends in *a consonant + vowel + consonant*, then we double the last consonant and add *-d.*

6. **With the verbs *fixed, snowed* and *enjoyed* in the past simple form, the last vowel is not doubled because:**

   a) the verb in the infinitive ends in *a vowel + consonant + i*
   b) the last syllable is not stressed or the verb ends in *-w, -x, -y*
   c) the verb in an infinitive has two syllables and ends in *a vowel + consonant + vowel*

2.5. PRONUNCIATION OF -ED ENDING

Regular verbs in the past simple tense and in the past participle form end in *-ed*, e.g. *want**ed**, travell**ed**, wait**ed**, prohibit**ed**, exaggerat**ed***. However, not all words ending in *-ed* are verbs. Adjectives can also end in *-ed*, e.g. *tired, shocked, amused, bored, tempted.*

Nevertheless, whether it is a verb or an adjective ending in *-ed*, the *-ed* is pronounced in one of three different ways:

a) If a word in its base form ends in the consonant *d* or *t*, the ending **-ed** is pronounced as /ɪd/, e.g.

- wai*t***ed** /ˈweɪtɪd/
- wan*t***ed** /ˈwɒntɪd/
- nee*d***ed** /ˈniːdɪd/

b) If the last vowel of a word in its base form is voiceless, the ending **-ed** is pronounced as /t/, e.g.

- talk**ed** /tɔːkt/
- kiss**ed** /kɪst/
- smok**ed** /sməʊkt/

c) If a word in its base form ends in a voiced sound, the ending **-ed** is pronounced as /d/, e.g.

- play**ed** /pleɪd/
- liv**ed** /lɪvd/
- clos**ed** /kləʊzd/

Remember that what is important is the last sound we hear in a verb or an adjective, not the letter it ends in. For example:

A. The verb <u>close</u> ends in the letter e, which is silent. However, in pronunciation, it ends in the sound /z/, which is a voiced sound. So when the ending -ed is added to it, the verb is pronounced /kləʊzd/.

B. The verb <u>fax</u> ends in the letter x, pronounced as /s/, which is a voiceless sound. So when we add the ending -ed to the verb fax the -ed ending is pronounced as /t/, which is /fakst/.

EXCEPTIONS

Some adjectives ending in **-ed** are not subject to the above rules and the ending **-ed** is pronounced as /ɪd/, /d/ or /t/, depending on the function they perform and even the context.

Pronunciation of **-ed** as /ɪd/:

- **aged** is pronounced /ˈeɪdʒɪd/ in the sense of *very old* when it comes before a noun, e.g. *her aged aunt - her very old aunt,*

- **beloved** is pronounced /bɪˈlʌvɪd/ when it comes before a noun in the sense of *loved very much*, e.g. *my beloved wife*, and when **beloved** functions as a noun, e.g. *she's my beloved,*

- **blessed** is pronounced /ˈblesɪd/ as an adjective in the sense of *holy, sacrificed* e.g. *the Blessed Virgin Mary,*

- **crooked** is pronounced /ˈkrʊkɪd/, e.g. *crooked smile,*

- **cursed** is pronounced /ˈkɜːsɪd/ as an adjective when cursed means *unpleasant, annoying* and comes before a noun, e.g. *This cursed illness – will I never be well again?*

- **dogged** is pronounced /ˈdɒgɪd/ as an adjective in the sense of *stubborn, obstinate*, e.g. *Everyone admires their dogged defence of the country.*

- **learned** is pronounced /ˈlɜːnɪd/ as an adjective in the sense of *knowledgeable, well educated*, e.g. *He's a learned scientist.*

- **naked** is pronounced /ˈneɪkɪd/ as an adjective in the sense of *not wearing any clothes, bare*, or *vulnerable*, e.g. *with the naked eye,*

- **ragged** is pronounced /ˈræɡɪd/ as an adjective in the sense of *frayed, sloppy*; e.g. *Look at that poor man wearing a ragged coat.*

- **sacred** is pronounced /ˈseɪkrɪd/ as an adjective in the sense of *holy, religious*, e.g. *a sacred cross*,

- **wicked** is pronounced /ˈwɪkɪd/ as an adjective in the sense of *vile, shameful, wonderful, horrible*, e.g. *She has a wicked sense of humour.*

- **wretched** is pronounced /ˈretʃɪd/ as an adjective in the sense of *unhappy, miserable, gloomy, pitiful*, e.g. *You look wretched.*

Pronunciation of **-ed** as /d/ or /t/:

- **aged** is pronounced /ˈeɪdʒd/, meaning of *the age of* and when it occurs as a verb in the sense of *getting older*, e.g. *She has a son aged /ˈeɪdʒd/ 12. He has aged /ˈeɪdʒd/ a lot in the last 2 years.*

- **beloved** is pronounced /bɪˈlʌvd/ when as an adjective it does not come immediately before the noun, e.g. *My father was beloved by everybody = my father was adored by everybody,*

- **blessed** is pronounced /ˈblest/ as a verb, e.g. *She blessed us.*

- **crooked** is pronounced /ˈkrʊkt/ as a verb, e.g. *He crooked his little finger.*

- **cursed** is pronounced /ˈkɜːst/ in the verb function, e.g. *The witch cursed them all* and also as an adjective meaning *suffering from a curse* e.g. *This castle is cursed.*

- **dogged** is pronounced /ˈdɒɡd/ in the verb function, e.g. *She dogged me all my life.*

- **learned** is pronounced /ˈlɜːnd/ as a verb, e.g. *I've learned a lot today.*

- **ragged** is pronounced /ˈræɡd/ as a verb in past simple/past participle form, e.g. *they ragged me about my shoes - they made fun of my shoes,*

- **wicked** is pronounced /ˈwɪkt/ in the verb function, e.g. *That fabric wicked away all moisture.*

QUIZ 5

1. **All words that end in *-ed* are verbs.**

   a) true
   b) false

2. **In the verbs *wanted, needed* and *hated* the ending *-ed* is pronounced as /ɪd/ because:**

   a) the verb in the infinitive ends in a voiced consonant
   b) the last vowel of the infinitive is soundless
   c) the verb in the infinitive ends in 'd' or 't'

3. **In the words *shopped, wished, looked* and *danced* the ending *-ed* is pronounced as:**

   a) /d/
   b) /ɪd/
   c) /t/

4. **In the words *called, tried, lived* and *loved* the ending *-ed* is pronounced as:**

   a) /ɪd/
   b) /d/
   c) /t/

5. **In the sentence *They ragged me about my shoes* the verb *ragged* is pronounced as:**

   a) /ˈrægd/
   b) /ˈrægɪd/
   c) /ˈrægt/

6. **The adjective *cursed* is pronounced as:**

   a) /ˈkɜːsɪd/
   b) /ˈkɜːsd/
   c) /ˈkɜːst/

2.6. THE PAST PARTICIPLE

The past participle is often called *the third form of a verb* or *the passive* or *perfect participle*. With a regular verb, the past participle is formed by adding -**ed**/-**d** to the infinitive.

With an irregular verb, on the other hand, the past participle has an irregular form. It is used to form the perfect tense (*present perfect, past perfect, future perfect*, etc.), the passive voice and it functions as an adjectival participle.

In the case of regular verbs, the past participle is formed according to the same rules as the past simple form (i.e. by adding *-ed/-d* to the infinitive), e.g.

	work	***play***	***cry***	***kiss***	***love***	***stop***
I	*work**ed***	*play**ed***	*cr**ied***	*kiss**ed***	*lov**ed***	*stopp**ed***
you	*work**ed***	*play**ed***	*cr**ied***	*kiss**ed***	*lov**ed***	*stopp**ed***
he	*work**ed***	*play**ed***	*cr**ied***	*kiss**ed***	*lov**ed***	*stopp**ed***
she	*work**ed***	*play**ed***	*cr**ied***	*kiss**ed***	*lov**ed***	*stopp**ed***
it	*work**ed***	*play**ed***	*cr**ied***	*kiss**ed***	*lov**ed***	*stopp**ed***
we	*work**ed***	*play**ed***	*cr**ied***	*kiss**ed***	*lov**ed***	*stopp**ed***
you	*work**ed***	*play**ed***	*cr**ied***	*kiss**ed***	*lov**ed***	*stopp**ed***
they	*work**ed***	*play**ed***	*cr**ied***	*kiss**ed***	*lov**ed***	*stopp**ed***

QUIZ 6

1. **The third form of the verb is otherwise known as the:**

   a) past participle
   b) perfect participle
   c) gerund form

2. **What ending is added to regular verbs to form the past participle?**

   a) *-de* or *-t*
   b) *-es* or *-s*

c) *-ed* or *-d*

3. The past participle of irregular verbs is formed in the same way as the past participle of regular verbs.

a) true
b) false

4. Form the past participle of the verb *play*. ______________

5. Form the past participle of the verb *smile*. ______________

6. The past participle of the verb *hope* is:

a) hopped
b) hoped
c) hopet

3. IRREGULAR VERBS

3.1. IRREGULAR VERB FORMS

Irregular verbs are a group where the past simple and past participle forms are not formed according to a fixed pattern, as in the case of regular verbs, but constitute varying forms that must be learned by heart.

An irregular verb, like the regular verbs described earlier, has five basic forms. These are respectively:

1. the base form, i.e. the infinitive
2. the third person singular present tense
3. the irregular past simple used to express the past
4. the irregular past participle, which is used to form the passive voice and the perfect tenses
5. verbs in the present participle form, i.e. with the characteristic *-ing* ending

The table below illustrates some irregular verbs and their forms.

infinitive	3rd person singular present tense	simple past	past participle	present participle
be	*is*	*was/were*	*been*	*being*
do	*does*	*did*	*done*	*doing*
go	*goes*	*went*	*gone*	*going*
have	*has*	*had*	*had*	*having*
grow	*grows*	*grew*	*grown*	*growing*
make	*makes*	*made*	*made*	*making*
put	*puts*	*put*	*put*	*putting*
buy	*buys*	*bought*	*bought*	*buying*
think	*thinks*	*thought*	*thought*	*thinking*

3.2. IRREGULAR VERB IN THE PRESENT TENSE

In the present simple, the irregular verb is only changed in the third person singular by adding -**s** or -**es** to the base form of the verb. With the other persons, the verb does not change and has the same form as the infinitive.

Thus, exactly the same rules apply as for regular verbs.

The exceptions are the verbs *be* and *have*, whose forms in the present tense are also irregular.

	be	***have***	***go***	***make***	***do***	***bring***
I	*am*	*have*	*go*	*make*	*do*	*bring*
you	*are*	*have*	*go*	*make*	*do*	*bring*
he	*is*	*has*	*goes*	*makes*	*does*	*brings*
she	*is*	*has*	*goes*	*makes*	*does*	*brings*
it	*is*	*has*	*goes*	*makes*	*does*	*brings*
we	*are*	*have*	*go*	*make*	*do*	*bring*
you	*are*	*have*	*go*	*make*	*do*	*bring*
they	*are*	*have*	*go*	*make*	*do*	*bring*

3.3. PAST SIMPLE AND PAST PARTICIPLE FORM OF AN IRREGULAR VERB

The general difference between regular and irregular verbs is that irregular verbs do not generally have an **-ed**/**-d** ending in the past simple and past participle forms, as in the case of regular verbs. The past simple and past participle forms must be learnt by heart.

Irregular verbs - both frequently and less frequently used (the list is extensive) - are discussed at greater length later in the text. This section covers, firstly, irregular verbs that have a different base form, past simple and past participle, secondly, irregular verbs that have the same past simple and past participle form, and thirdly, irregular verbs that have the same form in the infinitive, past simple and past participle.

Each verb is presented in three forms: infinitive, past simple and past participle. The form with the *-ing* ending, the so-called *gerund form*, is not discussed as this is a separate topic.

QUIZ 7

1. How is the third form of irregular verbs formed?

a) by adding the ending *-ed* or *-d* to the infinitive
b) no ending is necessary
c) the third form of an irregular verb does not exist

2. An irregular verb in the third person singular in the present simple tense has the ending:

a) *-es* or *-s*, depending on the verb
b) *-ed* or *-d* if it ends in *y*

3. The form *has* is:

a) the past participle of the verb *be*
b) the third singular form of *have* in the present tense
c) the past simple form of *have*

4. The third form (past participle) of the verb *be* is:

a) is/are
b) was
c) been

5. The irregular verb *buy* in the third person singular (he, she, it) in the present simple tense takes the form:

a) buyes
b) buys
c) buies

6. The pronunciation of the ending *-s* for irregular verbs in the third person singular in the present simple tense is the same as for regular verbs.

a) true
b) false

4. IRREGULAR VERBS WITH DIFFERENT FORMS IN THE PAST SIMPLE AND AS PAST PARTICIPLES

This section covers irregular verbs where:

a) the infinitive form, the past tense form and the past participle are different
b) the past tense form is different from the infinitive and the past participle is identical to the infinitive
c) the past tense form is the same as the infinitive and the past participle is different

infinitive	past simple	past participle
arise /əˈraɪz/	**arose** /əˈrəʊz/	**arisen** /əˈrɪzən/

to start to exist, to happen, to crop up, to stand up, to develop, to result from

He seized the opportunity as soon as it **arose**.

Their problems had **arisen** long before they decided to divorce.

Not even the best specialists knew where his unusual health condition **arose** from.

infinitive	past simple	past participle
awake /əˈweɪk/	**awoke** /əˈwəʊk/	**awoken** /əˈwəʊ.kən/

to wake up

Although the tiger was born in a zoo, its survival instincts **awoke** immediately after it was set free into the wild.

Diane **awoke** at the crack of dawn.

She was **awoken** in the middle of the night by the high-pitched screams of her neighbour.

infinitive	past simple	past participle
be /biː/	**was** /wɒz/ **were** /wɜːr/	**been** /biːn/

to exist, to be present

Where **were** you last Saturday?

She was disappointed to hear that she hadn't **been** offered the job.

The children **were** in the garden when I was preparing some snacks for them.

infinitive	past simple	past participle
bear /beər/	bore /bɔ:r/	born* /bɔ:n/ borne /bɔ:n/
to carry, to hold, to stand, to endure, to give birth, to incur (costs)		

** the verb **bear** /beər/ in the sense of "to give birth", in the past participle takes the form born /bɔ:n/, e.g. She was **born** in 1876. The verb **bear** /beər/ in its other senses has the form borne /bɔ:n/ as a past participle, e.g. The costs of commuting to work were **borne** by the employer.*

He was **born** in the jungle and raised by monkeys.

My landlord refused to repair the fridge and I **bore** the cost of the repairs myself.

About 80% of the tuition fees were **borne** by my university.

infinitive	past simple	past participle
beat /bi:t/	beat /bi:t/	beaten /ˈbi:.tən/
to defeat, to win, to whip, to beat sb up, to injure, to pulsate, to flap		

Our team was **beaten** by only 1 point.

I cannot believe that he **beat** his father senseless.

She **beat** the double cream for so long that she ended up with butter!

infinitive	past simple	past participle
become /bɪˈkʌm/	became /bɪˈkeɪm/	become /bɪˈkʌm/
to develop into, to grow into, to enhance, to suit, to fit**		

** with these meanings the verb **become** /bɪˈkʌm/ cannot be used in continuous form.*

Can you tell me why you **became** an artist?

My daughter has **become** a well-known cellist.

Elizabeth was tall and slender, so any long dress **became** her.

infinitive	past simple	past participle
beget /bɪˈget/	begot /bɪˈgɒt/ begat* /bɪˈgæt/	begot /bɪˈgɒt/ begotten* /bɪˈgɒtᵊn/
to cause, to bring about, to breed, to father		

** the verb **beget** /bɪˈget/ and its past simple and past participle form **begot** /bɪˈgɒt/ in the sense of "to cause something happen" is used in very formal language. **Beget** and its forms **begat** /bɪˈgæt//**begotten** /bɪˈgɒtᵊn/ in the sense of "to become the father of a child" is considered archaic and reserved for a biblical context.*

*Furthermore, in the present perfect or past perfect, **begot** is used. In interrogative sentences in the present perfect or past perfect tense, and in passive sentences, **begotten** is used.*

The Bible says that Adam **begat** Cain and Abel.

"There is no killing the suspicion that deceit has once **begotten**". – *George Eliot.*

According to the Bible, Abraham **begot** a second child at the age of 100, which would be considered biologically impossible these days – or a miracle.

infinitive	past simple	past participle
begin /bɪˈgɪn/	began /bɪˈgæn/	begun /bɪˈgʌn/
to start, to commence, to set about, to get going		

We've just **begun** to celebrate our 10th wedding anniversary.

Due to a fire at the school, the school year **began** almost three months later.

My Spanish teacher always **begins** lessons with icebreakers that help new students to get to know each other better.

infinitive	past simple	past participle
bespeak /bɪˈspiːk/	bespoke /bɪˈspəʊk/	bespoken /bɪˈspəʊkən/
to indicate, to imply, to denote		

Her generosity **bespeaks** her good nature.

Mr Franklin's speech **bespoke** his deep commitment to the affairs of the townspeople.

His latest diary entry has **bespoken** his true eloquence in the art of journaling.

infinitive	past simple	past participle
bite /baɪt/	bit /bɪt/	bitten /ˈbɪt.ən/
to grip with teeth, to chomp, to nibble, to sting, to gnaw, to pester		

I wanted to tell her what I thought of her, but I **bit** my tongue.

Have you ever been **bitten** by a snake?

Either rats or mice **bit** the cables and caused a short-circuit in the whole building.

infinitive	past simple	past participle
bestride* /bɪˈstraɪd/	bestrode /bɪˈstrəʊd/	bestridden /bɪˈstrɪdn/
to dominate, to straddle, to mount		

* *formal*

He **bestrode** the horse and galloped away.

The gangster boss already **bestrode** the entire district and nothing would stop him from taking over the whole city.

My dear young lady, we may be in Egypt but it's still completely inappropriate for a woman to **bestride** a camel in the fashion of a man. I insist you take a horse!

infinitive	past simple	past participle
bid* /bɪd/	bade /bæd/, /beɪd/ bid /bɪd/	bidden /ˈbɪdən/ bid /bɪd/
to command, to order, to wish		

**archaic/literary*

The police **bade/bid** everyone to evacuate the building immediately.

My father has **bidden/bid** me (to) tidy up my room.

I **bid** you all the best because you are my dearest friend.

infinitive	past simple	past participle
blow /bləʊ/	**blew** /blu:/	**blown** /bləʊn/
to gust, to rumble, to exhale, to use up (money), to spoil		

He **blew** it again! I would never again entrust anything to him.

The wind **blew** very hard the whole autumn.

Josh has **blown** all his money and now wants to borrow some from me.

infinitive	past simple	past participle
break /breɪk/	**broke** /brəʊk/	**broken** /ˈbrəʊ.kən/
to burst, to crash, to smash, to damage, to fracture, to interrupt, to stop, to overcome		

Who **broke** the window?

The old lady **broke** her leg after slipping on the kitchen floor.

My family have **broken** with tradition and decided to have goose instead of turkey this Christmas.

infinitive	past simple	past participle
browbeat /ˈbraʊ.bi:t/	**browbeat** /ˈbraʊ.bi:t/	**browbeaten** /ˈbraʊbi:tᵊn/
to harass, to intimidate, to frighten, to coerce		

I was **browbeaten** into signing the contract.

Nelson tried to **browbeat** me to get his way.

The police appeared to be on the side of the offender and **browbeat** me into testifying in his favour.

infinitive	past simple	past participle
choose /tʃuːz/	chose /tʃəʊz/	chosen /ˈtʃəʊ.zən/
to pick, to accept, to decide, to adopt		

I was placed in a difficult position and had to **choose** between the two men I loved.

They **chose** to share a flat and split all the bills.

He's **chosen** a lovely birthday gift for you.

infinitive	past simple	past participle
come /kʌm/	came /keɪm/	come /kʌm/
to arrive, to approach, to happen, to appear, to show up, to stem		

He **came** a long way.

Just **come** with us and enjoy yourself.

The parcel hasn't **come** yet.

Simon **came** to help me out last week.

infinitive	past simple	past participle
do /duː/	did /dɪd/	done /dʌn/
to perform, to realise, to cheat, to study, to get on, to prepare, to behave, to decorate, to solve, to be adequate, to produce		

Whoever **did** that must face the consequences.

This incident has nothing to **do** with me.

I've **done** a few French lessons now, but can still only order a cup of tea!

What **did** you do with my old clothes?

infinitive	past simple	past participle
draw /drɔː/	drew /druː/	drawn /drɔːn/
to pull, to drag, to withdraw, to attract, to sketch, to tie		

I've **drawn** out 200 dollars. Is that enough?

What did you **draw**?

He **drew** a caricature of me that was shockingly similar.

Samantha had enormous charisma, and always **drew** the attention of everyone around her.

infinitive	past simple	past participle
drink /drɪŋk/	drank /dræŋk/	drunk /drʌŋk/
to swallow liquids, to booze, to accept a bribe (slang)		

He's **drunk** too much beer.

She **drank** a glass of water.

He **drinks** only beetroot juice because it's apparently very healthy.

infinitive	past simple	past participle
drive /draɪv/	drove /drəʊv/	driven /ˈdrɪv.ən/
to go by car, to travel by car, to give somebody a lift, to motivate		

Sheila **drove** me mad and that was the reason I left her.

He **drove** under the influence of alcohol.

They've been **driven** by a desire to maximise profit.

infinitive	past simple	past participle
eat /iːt/	ate /et/, /eɪt/	eaten /ˈiːtᵊn/
to consume food, to dog, to oppress		

I **ate** the whole cake.

What would you like to **eat** for breakfast?

Have you **eaten** anything today?

Guilt over causing a colleague's death **ate** into him every day.

infinitive	past simple	past participle
fall /fɔːl/	fell /fel/	fallen /ˈfɔː.lən/
to go down, to drop, to decrease, to diminish, to slip into, to take place		

Dan **fell** and broke his wrist.

I like the way your hair **falls** over your shoulders.

Easter **fell** late last year.

After the storm, I saw that a massive tree had **fallen** less than a metre away from my car.

It's not uncommon to **fall** into depression after losing one's job.

infinitive	past simple	past participle
fly /flaɪ/	flew /fluː/	flown /fləʊn/
to aviate, to operate an aeroplane, to be on the wing		

They **flew** to Canada last Tuesday.

Have you ever **flown** a kite?

A flock of wild geese has just **flown** over our house.

Do you want to **fly** back to Paris or take the train?

infinitive	past simple	past participle
forbear* /fɔːˈbeər/	forbore /fɔːˈbɔːr/	forborne /fɔːˈbɔːn/
to abstain from, to avoid doing something		

**formal*

Nevertheless, I respect my privacy and I **forbear** anyone to interfere with my intimate affairs.

I **forbore** to say that Mr Braithwaite had only married my cousin for her money. – said Mrs Scarlett.

It is too early to celebrate our success and that is why I have **forborne** giving any further details on this matter.

infinitive	past simple	past participle
forbid /fəˈbɪd/	forbade /fəˈbæd/, /fəˈbeɪd/	forbidden /fəˈbɪd.ən/
to ban, to prohibit, to make something impossible		

She was **forbidden** from meeting her friends.

England's Parliament **forbade** the celebration of Christmas in 1647.

Lack of money **forbids** them from going to university.

infinitive	past simple	past participle
forego/forgo* /fɔːˈgəʊ/	forewent /fɔːˈwɛnt/ forwent /fɔːˈwɛnt/	foregone /ˌfɔː.gɒn/ forgone /ˌfɔː.gɒn/
to do without, to give up, to bow out of something		

**formal*

He has **foregone/forgone** holidays abroad in order to save up for a house.

If you want to lose weight, you have to **forgo/forego** sweets.

Although the princess could live in the king's palace and have everything she desired, she **forewent/forwent** such luxury and lived in a shack in the woods with a simple woodcutter whom she loved.

infinitive	past simple	past participle
foresee /fəˈsiː/	foresaw /fɔːˈsɔː/	foreseen /fɔːˈsiːn/
to predict, to forecast		

She **foresaw** many important events, most of which came true.

No one could have **foreseen** that the bank would go bankrupt.

I didn't **foresee** that happening.

infinitive	past simple	past participle
forswear* /fɔːˈsweər/	forswore /fɔːˈswɔː/	forsworn /fɔːˈswɔːn/
to deny, to renounce, to reject		

**formal/literary*

Brad has **forsworn** the criminal life he has been leading for many years.

St Francis of Assisi abandoned his home and family and **forswore** all his wealth.

The drug manufacturer has **forsworn** the use of a potentially detrimental chemical that may lead to brain cancer.

infinitive	past simple	past participle
forget /fəˈget/	forgot /fəˈgɒt/	forgotten /fəˈgɒtn/
to not remember, to banish		

I’d completely **forgotten** about the meeting.

Don’t **forget** to water the plants when we’re away.

She **forgot** to take her passport and wasn’t able to cross the border.

infinitive	past simple	past participle
forgive /fə'gɪv/	forgave /fə'geɪv/	forgiven /fə'gɪvn/
to condone, to remit		

I **forgave** him for what he’d done to me.

She doesn’t **forgive** people easily.

I don't think Luiza has ever quite **forgiven** her husband for cheating on her.

infinitive	past simple	past participle
forsake* /fə'seɪk/	forsook /fə'sʊk/	forsaken /fə'seɪkən/
to abandon, to desert, to cease		

**literary/formal*

After the love of my life **forsook** me, my world collapsed and I was never again able to lose my heart to another man.

I beg you to not **forsake** me! (*literary*)

Arthur was an oil executive but has **forsaken** such a career to become a priest. (*very formal*)

infinitive	past simple	past participle
freeze /fri:z/	froze /frəʊz/	frozen /'frəʊzən/
to refrigerate, to chill, to crash, to hang		

The lake has **frozen** during the night.

My mum buys all types of fruit in season and **freezes** them for winter.

My phone screen **froze** and I couldn’t press any buttons.

infinitive	past simple	past participle
give /gɪv/	gave /geɪv/	given /gɪvn/

to provide, to get something in, to present, to allow, to pass something on, to organise

A: What did you **give** her? B: I **gave** her roses.

We haven't been **given** permission to do that.

It was you who **gave** me the flu.

infinitive	past simple	past participle
go /gəʊ/	went /went/	gone /gɒn/

to move, to leave, to pass away, to sell out, to attend, to match, to progress

I'm sorry, but all the buns are **gone**.

Don't **go** yet. Stay a bit longer.

My family **went** for a picnic last Saturday.

infinitive	past simple	past participle
grow /grəʊ/	grew /gruː/	grown /grəʊn/

to evolve, to get bigger, to get taller, to cultivate, to rise, to sprout

Has Mike **grown** a beard?

Last summer we **grew** cherry tomatoes in the garden.

My hair **grows** very fast, so I have to have my haircut at least twice a month.

infinitive	past simple	past participle
handwrite /ˈhændraɪt/	handwrote /ˈhændrəʊt/	handwritten /ˈhændrɪtn/

to write by hand

The manuscript was completely **handwritten**.

I **handwrote** the list of names.

When she **handwrites** a letter nobody can read it.

infinitive	past simple	past participle
hide /haɪd/	hid /hɪd/	hidden /hɪdn/

to secrete, to conceal, to stash, to camouflage

I can't remember where I **hid** my diary.

Where have you **hidden** the children's Christmas gifts?

Why do we **hide** secrets from other people?

infinitive	past simple	past participle
interweave /ˌɪn.təˈwiːv/	interwove /ˌɪn.təˈwəʊv/	interwoven /ˌɪn.təˈwəʊvən/

to entangle, to entwine, to knit something together

These two subplots in the book are skilfully **interwoven**.

She **interwove** silk thread with gold.

These two unsolved cases are somehow inextricably **interwoven** with each other.

infinitive	past simple	past participle
know /nəʊ/	knew /njuː/	known /nəʊn/

to be aware of somebody/something, to be familiar with, to realise, to learn, to experience

How long have you **known** each other?

My mum doesn't **know** how to use a smartphone.

They **knew** nothing about it.

infinitive	past simple	past participle
lade* /leɪd/	laded /leɪdɪd/	laden /ˈleɪdᵊn/ laded /leɪdɪd/

to load, to pile, to freight

* *archaic*

Her shopping bag, as usual, was **laden/laded** with groceries and fruit.

The tree was **laden/laded** with fruit.

If the truck hadn't been **laden/laded** with so many goods, it wouldn't have caused the accident.

infinitive	past simple	past participle
lie /laɪ/	lay /leɪ/ lied * /laɪd/	lain /leɪn/ lied * /laɪd/
*to recline, to be situated on, to rest, to be laid to rest, to not tell the truth**		

** the verb **lie** /laɪ/ is also a regular verb, meaning "to not tell the truth". Its past simple and past participle form is **lied** /laɪd/, e.g.: She has **lied** to everyone.*

He has **lain** in bed all day.

Here **lies** my great-great-grandfather – a war hero.

The problems **lay** in our lack of mutual understanding.

He always **lies** to me.

The dog **lay** on a cushion by the fire.

infinitive	past simple	past participle
mistake /mɪˈsteɪk/	mistook /mɪˈstʊk/	mistaken /mɪˈsteɪkən/
to confuse, to mix somebody/something up, to make an error, to misunderstand		

You're **mistaken** – he had nothing to do with it.

I beg your pardon, I **mistook** you for someone else.

You can't **mistake** my house – it's painted bright yellow.

infinitive	past simple	past participle
misspeak* /ˌmɪsˈspiːk/	misspoke /ˌmɪsˈspəʊk/	misspoken /ˌmɪsˈspəʊkn/
to express oneself unclearly or incorrectly, to speak misleadingly or deceptively		

the verb **misspeak /ˌmɪsˈspiːk/ is mainly used in American English.*

I was distracted and I may have **misspoken**.

She claimed that she **misspoke** but I think it was a deliberate lie.

Natalie obviously **misspoke** when she called her husband by their son's name.

infinitive	past simple	past participle
mow /məʊ/	mowed /məʊd/	mown /məʊn/ mowed /məʊd/
to cut, to trim, to crop		

He hasn't **mowed/mown** the lawn yet.

Don't **mow** the grass in the morning when it's covered with dew.

The grass had grown quite a lot, so I **mowed** it yesterday.

infinitive	past simple	past participle
outdo /ˌaʊtˈduː/	outdid /ˌaʊtˈdɪd/	outdone /ˌaʊtˈdʌn/
to better, to surpass, to excel		

Shaun always tried to **outdo** his cousins.

Madonna has **outdone** herself – it was one of her best performances.

She **outdid** the other contestants to win the finals.

infinitive	past simple	past participle
outdrink /ˌaʊtˈdrɪŋk/	outdrank /ˌaʊtˈdræŋk/	outdrunk /ˌaʊtˈdrʌŋk/
to drink more than somebody else		

Terry **outdrank** me at the party.

I've **outdrunk** you, so you lose the bet.

The guys got completely hammered after they decided to **outdrink** each other.

infinitive	past simple	past participle
outdrive /ˌaʊtˈdraɪv/	outdrove /ˌaʊtˈdrəʊv/	outdriven /ˌaʊtˈdrɪvᵊn/
to drive a vehicle faster than, to drive a golf ball further than		

Every golfer practices to **outdrive** their competitors.

Alec has **outdriven** everybody else – and it was the furthest shot in his golfing career.

Peterson **outdrove** Sanders and thereby won the race.

infinitive	past simple	past participle
outgrow /ˌaʊtˈɡrəʊ/	outgrew /ˌaʊtˈɡruː/	outgrown /ˌaʊtˈɡrəʊn/
to grow too fast or faster than, to grow out of something, to exceed (weight/capacity)		

I bought these trousers for my 12-year-old son five months ago, but he has already **outgrown** them.

Josh **outgrew** his older brother a few months ago and is now a centimetre taller.

Children **outgrow** their clothes and shoes very quickly.

infinitive	past simple	past participle
overcome /ˌəʊ.vəˈkʌm/	overcame /ˌəʊ.vəˈkeɪm/	overcome /ˌəʊ.vəˈkʌm/
to defeat, to conquer, to overwhelm, to surmount, to tackle, to overpower		

People sometimes struggle to **overcome** the obstacles in their lives.

I've finally **overcome** my social anxiety.

A panic attack **overcame** her and she couldn't think clearly.

infinitive	past simple	past participle
overdo /ˌəʊ.vəˈduː/	overdid /ˌəʊ.vəˈdɪd/	overdone /ˌəʊ.vəˈdʌn/
to exaggerate, to overestimate, to overcook, to go overboard with something		

I don't like my steak **overdone**.

Don't **overdo** the drinks - two beers each will be enough.

I always thought Mark Rothko **overdid** the black in his pictures - it makes them depressing.

infinitive	past simple	past participle
overdraw /ˌəʊ.vəˈdrɔː/	overdrew /ˌəʊvəˈdruː/	overdrawn /ˌəʊvəˈdrɔːn/
to exceed a bank account balance by taking out too much money		

Have you **overdrawn** your credit card limit this month?

I **overdrew** my account by €5 and that's why the payment didn't go through.

Are there any fees if I **overdraw** my account?

The main protagonist in the book was **overdrawn** and therefore unconvincing as a character.

infinitive	past simple	past participle
overeat /əʊ.vəˈiːt/	overate /əʊ.vəˈet/, /əʊ.vəˈeɪt/	overeaten /əʊ.vəˈiːtn/
to eat too much, to consume too much food, to gorge oneself		

You're not supposed to **overeat** before going to bed.

I **overate** at the wedding reception and now feel sick.

Some people suffering from depression tend to either **overeat** or undereat.

infinitive	past simple	past participle
overfly /əʊ.vəˈflaɪ/	overflew /əʊ.vəˈfluː/	overflown /əʊ.vəˈfləʊn/
to fly over something, to fly beyond		

We've just **overflown** the city.

The plane mistakenly **overflew** prohibited airspace.

A fighter pilot is always in danger when they overfly hostile territory.

infinitive	past simple	past participle
override /əʊ.vəˈraɪd/	overrode /əʊ.vəˈrəʊd/	overridden /əʊ.vəˈrɪdn/
to outweigh, to overrule, to ignore, to disregard, to set on automatic pilot		

The fireman **overrode** the building's automatic sprinkler system in order to shut it down.

The Supreme Court has **overridden** an earlier decision by a High Court judge.

The Senate voted to **override** the president's veto last Tuesday.

infinitive	past simple	past participle
overrun /ˌəʊ.vəˈrʌn/	overran /ˌəʊ.vəˈræn/	overrun /ˌəʊ.vəˈrʌn/
to subjugate, to raid, to invade, to go beyond, to infest, to exceed		

Poland was **overrun** by the Mongols in 1241.

The exam **overran** by 30 minutes.

They were planning to **overrun** the country.

infinitive	past simple	past participle
oversee /ˌəʊ.vəˈsiː/	**oversaw** /ˌəʊ.vəˈsɔː/	**overseen** /ˌəʊ.vəˈ siːn/
to supervise, to control		

It's your responsibility to **oversee** production.

Mike used to be the Chief Financial Officer (CFO) and so always **oversaw** the budget.

Monica has **overseen** the process from the very beginning.

infinitive	past simple	past participle
overtake /ˌəʊvəˈteɪk/	**overtook** /ˌəʊvəˈtʊk/	**overtaken** /ˌəʊvəˈteɪkən/
to overhaul, to catch up with, to overwhelm		

If he hadn't **overtaken** the other car, he wouldn't have caused the accident.

It's dangerous to **overtake** on a bend.

A sudden pang of grief **overtook** her.

infinitive	past simple	past participle
overthrow /ˌəʊvəˈθrəʊ/	**overthrew** /ˌəʊvəˈθruː/	**overthrown** /ˌəʊ.vəˈθrəʊn/
to pull down, to bring something down, to demolish, to destroy		

The dictator was finally **overthrown** after his people rose up against him.

The Gambia **overthrew** its monarchy in 1970.

A rumour has it that they want to **overthrow** the government.

infinitive	past simple	past participle
partake* /pɑːˈteɪk/	**partook** /pɑːˈtʊk/	**partaken** /pɑːˈteɪkən/
to eat, to drink, to consume, to participate in, to take part in		

**formal/old-fashioned*

Sir Galahad, would you care to **partake** of a pheasant with me tonight?

He **partook** in the jousting competition and was toppled from his horse.

The Queen has **partaken** in many interesting events this year.

I **partook** of a candlelit dinner at the palace and I must say it was delicious.

infinitive	past simple	past participle
redo /riːˈduː/	redid /riːˈdɪd /	redone /riːˈdʌn /

to do something again, to renew, to redecorate, to remake

You'll have to **redo** your essay. I found a lot of mistakes.

I've **redone** my first survey because the questions were too complicated.

We're having the bathroom **redone**.

infinitive	past simple	past participle
redraw /ˌriːˈdrɔː/	redrew /ˌriːˈdruː/	redrawn /ˌriːˈdrɔːn /

to alter the borders of a country/region, to revise

After the Second World War, the map of Europe was **redrawn**.

She **redrew** her picture because she didn't like the first attempt.

It was necessary to **redraw** the local parish boundaries.

infinitive	past simple	past participle
rerun /ˌriːˈrʌn/	reran /ˌriːˈræn/	rerun /ˌriːˈrʌn/

to broadcast a movie or programme again, to renew, to organise or do something again

The competition had to be **rerun** after cheating was discovered in the first round.

Is the BBC going to **rerun** old episodes of that terrible comedy?

The country clerk **reran** the municipal elections last Thursday.

My favourite childhood Disney cartoon, "One Hundred and One Dalmatians", was **rerun** 🇺🇸 **/repeated** 🇬🇧 on TV yesterday afternoon.

infinitive	past simple	past participle
retake /ˌriːˈteɪk/	retook /ˌriːˈtʊk /	retaken /ˌriːˈteɪkən /

to resit, to take a test again, to take control of something again

I have to **retake** an English exam in May.

He **retook** his maths exam twice.

All the tests we've carried out are invalid and will have to be **retaken**.

infinitive	past simple	past participle
rewrite /ˌriːˈraɪt/	rewrote /ˌriːˈrəʊt /	rewritten /ˌriːˈrɪtn /
to write something again differently, to correct, to edit		

Her essay was badly written, so her teacher told her to **rewrite** it.

This article must be **rewritten** as it doesn't reflect the facts.

I **rewrote** all the paragraphs. Could you check them?

infinitive	past simple	past participle
ride /raɪd/	rode /rəʊd/	ridden /rɪdn/
to travel on (a horse, a bike, a bus)		

Have you **ridden** a horse before?

Can she **ride** a bike?

I **rode** / **went** to work by train in the morning.

As a child, Susan often **rode** on her father's shoulders when they went for a walk.

infinitive	past simple	past participle
ring /rɪŋ/	rang /ræŋ/ ringed * /rɪŋd/	rung /raŋ/ ringed * /rɪŋd/
to call, to buzz, to sound, to encircle, to surround**		

* *the verb* ***ring*** */rɪŋ/ also means "to surround", "to encircle", "to outline with a circle" and in this sense is a regular verb whose past simple and past participle form is* ***ringed*** */rɪŋd/, e.g. The lake is* ***ringed*** *with tall evergreen conifers. = The lake is surrounded by tall evergreen conifers.*

The phone **rang** several times, but no one was there when I picked up.

Have you **rung** me today?

The church bells **ring** on the hour.

infinitive	past simple	past participle
rise /raɪz/	rose /rəʊz/	risen /rɪzn/
to stand up, to get up, to go up, to climb		

The plane **rose** sharply up into the air.

What time does the sun **rise**?

Oil prices have **risen** by 10 %.

infinitive	past simple	past participle
rive* /raɪv/	rived /raɪvd/	riven /ˈrɪvᵊn/ rived /raɪvd/

to split, to tear/rip apart, to rend, to splinter

**literary/archaic*

The verb **rive** is uncommon in modern English usage.

The Lady of Shalott's heart was **riven** with distress when her mirror cracked.

The jury of the talent show was **rived** by bitter disagreement of which contestants performed the song best.

infinitive	past simple	past participle
run /rʌn/	ran /ræn/	run /rʌn/

to speed, to race, to hurry, to flee, to direct a company, to publish, to be on

Don't **run**! Just walk slowly.

She has **run** away from home and we're trying to find her.

I **ran** my own business.

infinitive	past simple	past participle
saw /sɔ:/	sawed /sɔ:d/	sawn /sɔ:n/ sawed /sɔ:d/

to cut with a saw

Pete **sawed** the branch in half.

He wanted to **saw** the board into pieces.

I've **sawn** several boards.

infinitive	past simple	past participle
see /siː/	**saw** /sɔː/	**seen** /siːn/

to perceive, to observe, to watch, to spot, to understand, to find out, to notice, to visit, to come across

Have I **seen** you somewhere before?
Ok, I **see.** I'll have to do it myself, then.
Dave **saw** his ex-girlfriend yesterday.

infinitive	past simple	past participle
sew /səʊ/	**sewed** /səʊd/	**sewed** /səʊd/ **sewn** /səʊn/

to stitch, to run something up

My mother taught me how to **sew**.
I **sewed** this dress by hand.
The edges of this fabric must be **sewn/sewed** with black thread.

infinitive	past simple	past participle
shake /ʃeɪk/	**shook** /ʃʊk/	**shaken** /ˈʃeɪkən/

to tremble, to shiver, to rock, to shock

He **shook** the palm tree until a coconut fell down.
Residents were **shaken** to hear of the murder in their street.
Her hands begin to **shake** when she is stressed.

infinitive	past simple	past participle
show /ʃəʊ/	**showed** /ʃəʊd/	**shown** /ʃəʊn/ **showed*** /ʃəʊd/

to demonstrate, to display, to guide, to usher, to express, to transmit

* *the past participle form* ***showed*** */ʃəʊd/ is used extremely rarely.*

I **showed** her some works by a young and upcoming painter.
Could you **show** me where the bus station is on the map?

I've already **shown** you how the machine works, haven't I?

infinitive	past simple	past participle
shrink /ʃrɪŋk/	shrank /ʃræŋk/ shrunk /ʃrʌŋk/	shrunk /ʃrʌŋk/

to dwindle, to decrease, to lessen, to cringe, to flinch

Her dress **shrank** when she washed it in hot water.

The doctor told me that, despite the treatment, the tumour hadn't **shrunk** any further.

Edward always **shrinks** away from large dogs.

infinitive	past simple	past participle
shrive* /ʃraɪv/	shrove /ʃrəʊv/	shriven /ˈʃrɪvᵊn/

to set free from guilt, to absolve, to atone, to confess one's sins

* *the verb **shrive** /ʃraɪv/ is considered old-fashioned.*

Before battle a priest **shrove** the king in order that he not die unconfessed.

Mum, what did that old priest mean by saying "young boy, all your sins will be **shriven**?"

Certainly, it was a monastic vocation and all of them had to **shrive** themselves.

infinitive	past simple	past participle
sing /siŋ/	sang /sæŋ/	sung /saŋ/

to chant, to whistle, to chirp, to rat, to inform on

She **sang** the song beautifully.

He's **sung** this song thousands of times in his career.

I love listening to the crickets **sing** in the evening.

infinitive	past simple	past participle
sink /sɪŋk/	sank /sæŋk/	sunk /saŋk/

to drown, to founder, to go down, to go under, to get worse, to drop

The ferry **sank** in the middle of the river.
If you don't add baking powder, the cake will **sink** in the middle.
My spirits have **sunk** because our team lost.

infinitive	past simple	past participle
sky-write /skaɪ'raɪt /	sky-wrote /skaɪ'rəʊt /	sky-written /skaɪˈrɪt.ən /
to write a message in the sky with smoke emitted from an aircraft		

The light aircraft flew over us and **sky-wrote** "Happy New Year".
I couldn't see the **sky-written** message because of the fog.
My boyfriend hired a plane to **sky-write** "Will you marry me, Jessie?"

infinitive	past simple	past participle
slay* /sleɪ/	slew /slu:/ slayed** /sleɪd/	slain /sleɪn/ slayed** /sleɪd/
to kill, to slaughter, to murder, to eliminate, to impress, to amuse		

* *archaic/literary*

*** *the verb* **slay** */sleɪ/ can also be regular with the meaning "to delight", "amuse" (colloquial), in which case its past simple form and past participle is* ***slayed*** */sleɪd/, e.g.*

That old comedy really **slayed** me. - That old comedy really made me laugh.

The King has **slain** his arch enemy.
Legend has it that St George **slew** the dragon.
How easy is it to **slay** a vampire?

infinitive	past simple	past participle
smite* /smaɪt/	smote /sməʊt/	smitten /ˈsmɪtᵊn/
to bang, to smash, to hit hard, to defeat		

* *archaic/literary*

We will **smite** our enemies.
Arthur **smote** each of his foes with the sword that had crowned him king.

Although they have been **smitten** with their own weapon they haven't acknowledged their fears and sustained their courage in their fight in the name of Jesus – claims Roger Davies, an influential American evangelist.

infinitive	past simple	past participle
sow /səʊ/	sowed /səʊd/	sown /səʊn/ sowed /səʊd/
to plant, to seed, to insinuate		

They'll **sow** the field with potatoes.

The farmer **sowed** the sunflower seeds in several rows.

Her actions have **sown/sowed** many doubts in my mind.

infinitive	past simple	past participle
speak /spiːk/	spoke /spəʊk/	spoken /ˈspəʊ.kən/
to talk, to tell, to say, to have a word, to give a speech, to give a lecture		

Can I **speak** to your manager immediately, please?

Tim is definitely at work today. I've just **spoken** to him.

He **spoke** for two hours but it was worth listening to him.

infinitive	past simple	past participle
spring /sprɪŋ/	sprang /spræŋ/ 🇬🇧 🇺🇸 sprung /sprʌŋ/ 🇺🇸	sprung /sprʌŋ/
to jump, to bounce, to recoil, to leap aside, to show up unexpectedly		

My cat **sprang** from my arms onto the floor.

This new art movement has **sprung** from Expressionism.

Where did he **spring** from? I didn't see him come in.

infinitive	past simple	past participle
steal /stiːl/	stole /stəʊl/	stolen /ˈstəʊlən/
to take something without permission, to lift, to pinch, to sneak (up)		

He was caught trying to **steal** a car.

The number of bicycles **stolen** each year has risen.

He seemed innocent, but it turned out that it was he who **stole** the money.

infinitive	past simple	past participle
stink /stɪŋk/	stank /stæŋk/ stunk /stʌŋk/	stunk /stʌŋk/
to reek, to pong, to be worth nothing		

He always **stinks** of beer and cigarettes.

Without any doubt, the concert **stank**.

The flat had **stunk** of fried fish until they opened the windows.

infinitive	past simple	past participle
strew /stru:/	strewed /stru:d/	strewn /stru:n/ strewed /stru:d/
to litter, to scatter, to swamp		

The main square was **strewn/strewed** with litter after the concert.

A sudden gust of wind **strewed** leaves all over the surface of the swimming pool.

My father hates it when I **strew** my books around the house.

infinitive	past simple	past participle
stride /straɪd/	strode /strəʊd/	stridden /ˈstridən/
to walk with long steps		

He **strode** purposefully along the road.

Matt has just **stridden** out of the room to confront his boss.

He's only 9 but he likes to **stride** about like a real soldier.

infinitive	past simple	past participle
strive* /straɪv/	strove /strəʊv/ strived /straɪvd/	striven /ˈstrɪvn/ strived /straɪvd/
to try hard, to attempt, to aspire, to aim at		

* *formal*

She **strove/strived** to please everyone, not understanding that it wasn't the way to get everyone to like her.

He **strives** to be perfect, but it's not possible.

We've **striven/strived** for equality all our lives.

infinitive	past simple	past participle
swear /sweə/	swore /swɔː/	sworn /swɔːn/
to curse, to vow, to declare		

He **swears** like a sailor.

She **swore** loyalty to the company.

I've **sworn** to tell the truth.

infinitive	past simple	past participle
swell /swel/	swelled /sweld/	swollen /ˈswəʊlən/
to puff up, to expand, to bloat, to surge		

My ankle has **swollen** up.

The wind **swelled** and began to blow hard.

The river always **swells** after a rainstorm.

infinitive	past simple	past participle
swim /swɪm/	swam /swæm/	swum /swʌm/
to bathe, to float, to whirl		

I don't believe that he **swam** across the lake.

I've just **swum** 40 lengths of the pool and feel shattered.

Where did you learn to **swim**?

infinitive	past simple	past participle
take /teɪk/	took /tʊk/	taken /ˈteɪkən/
to grab, to seize, to bring, to stand, to note, to last, to call for, to take on		

Have you decided yet if you want to **take** the job?

It **took** us almost a month to refurbish the house after the flood.

Have you **taken** my newspaper? I can't find it anywhere.

infinitive	past simple	past participle
tear /tɛə/	tore /tɔ:/	torn /tɔ:n/

to rip, to snag, to yank, to jerk, to scratch, to pull apart, to rush

She has **torn** her dress on a fence.

The boys **tore** across the playground.

A thief tried to **tear** a handbag off a woman's shoulder in the street.

infinitive	past simple	past participle
thrive /θraɪv/	thrived /θraɪvd/ (UK, US) throve* /θrəʊv/ (US)	thrived /θraɪvd/ (UK, US) thriven* /ˈθrɪvᵊn/ (US)

to prosper, to dow, to flourish, to bloom

* *the past simple form* ***throve*** */θrəʊv/ and the past participle* ***thriven*** */ˈθrɪvᵊn/ in American English is much less commonly used than* ***thrived*** */θraɪvd/.*

The bakery will have to increase its range if it wants to **thrive**.

My orchids have **thrived** since I placed them in indirect sunlight.

Some businesses **thrived,** while others struggled during the economic crisis.

infinitive	past simple	past participle
throw /θrəʊ/	threw /θru:/	thrown /θrəʊn/

to toss, to hurl, to slap, to fling, to baffle, to organise

I couldn't be bothered to go downstairs, so I **threw** the key to him out of the window.

Don't you dare **throw** stones at those birds.

Her response has completely **thrown** me. I now don't know what to do.

infinitive	past simple	past participle
tread /tred/	trod /trɒd/ treaded /tredid/	trodden /trɒdn/ trod /trɒd/ treaded /tredid/

to step, to stamp

Sadly, I'm not a good dancer - I tend to **tread** on my partner's feet.

She didn't see the cat and accidentally **trod** on its tail.

Oh, no! Look what I've **trodden/trod** in!

infinitive	past simple	past participle
undergo /ˌʌn.dəˈgəʊ/	underwent /ˌʌn.dəˈwent /	undergone /ˌʌn.dəˈ gɒn /

to go through, to endure, to bear, to withstand

She doesn't want to **undergo** surgery because she is afraid of general anaesthetic.

Last year my father **underwent** an operation for a tumour in his bladder.

In recent months she has **undergone** many changes in her professional and private life.

infinitive	past simple	past participle
underlie* /ˌʌn.dəˈlaɪ/	underlay /ˌʌndərˈleɪ /	underlain /ˌʌndəˈleɪn/

to be placed under, to be at the basis of something

* *formal*

"In every area of our lives, the three things that most need to be shared are resentments that have built up, the unmet needs and demands that **underlie** those resentments, and appreciations." – *Jack Canfield.*

Commitment and hard work **underlay** his success.

Scientists cannot explain what happened to the groundwater that previously **underlay** the surface of this geological area.

infinitive	past simple	past participle
undertake /ˌʌndəˈteɪk/	**undertook** /ˌʌndəˈtʊk/	**undertaken** /ˌʌndəˈteɪkən/
to take on, to embark on, to oblige		

I **undertook** extra work in order to pay off my debts.

She has **undertaken** to arrange all formalities for the trip to China.

The post requires you to **undertake** a number of duties.

infinitive	past simple	past participle
underwrite /ˌʌn.dərˈaɪt/	**underwrote** /ˌʌn.dərˈrəʊt /	**underwritten** /ˌʌn.dərˈrɪt.ən /
to guarantee, to endorse, to insure, to sign		

The two pharmaceutical companies have **underwritten** the project with a grant of €3 million.

Another bank **underwrote** my loan - not my own bank.

You must **underwrite** this document in front of the notary public. (*old usage*)

If you can't afford to pay in full for your car, our company can offer you a loan, which we **underwrite** it with a well-known bank.

infinitive	past simple	past participle
undo /ʌnˈduː/	**undid** /ʌnˈdɪd/	**undone** /ʌnˈdʌn/
to unfasten, to unbutton, to reverse, to cancel, to ruin		

Despite the turbulence, she **undid** her seat belt and tried to use the aircraft's toilet.

How can you possibly **undo** all the damage you have done?

What is done cannot be **undone**.

infinitive	past simple	past participle
unfreeze /ʌnˈfriːz/	**unfroze** /ʌnˈfrəʊz/	**unfrozen** /ʌnˈfrəʊzn/
to defrost, to thaw, to unblock (assets)		

Derek has just **unfrozen** the pipe with a blowtorch – so now we have water!

The meat wasn't actually fresh but had been **unfrozen** before use.

The bank is refusing to **unfreeze** assets belonging to customers associated with money laundering.

The strong sunlight **unfroze** the ground later that morning.

infinitive	past simple	past participle
wake /weɪk/	woke /wəʊk/ waked* /weɪkd/ 🇺🇸	woken /ˈwəʊ.kən/ waked* /weɪkd/ 🇺🇸
to awake, to get up, to arouse		

** in American English you can come across **waked** /weɪkd/ as the past simple and past participle forms.*

Could you **wake** me at 5 tomorrow?

I **woke** up at sunrise.

Don't make her angry, she has just **woken** up.

infinitive	past simple	past participle
weave /wiːv/	wove /wəʊv/ weaved* /wiːvd/	woven /ˈwəʊvən/ weaved* /wiːvd/
to knit, to intertwine, to spin, to plot, to move along obstacles		

** the verb **weave** /wiːv/ in the sense of "to move along", "to sneak through" is regular and takes the form **weaved** /wiːvd/ in past simple and past participle. With other meanings it takes the irregular forms **wove** /wəʊv/ and **woven** /ˈwəʊvən/, e.g.*

She has **woven** many replica tapestries for refurbished castles.

My Uncle Hubert **wove** the best stories.

My grandmother knew how to **weave** baskets from rushes.

My grandmother **wove** a woollen scarf for me.

A bizarre creature **weaved** between the trees and vanished without trace.

infinitive	past simple	past participle
wear /weə/	wore /wɔː/	worn /wɔːn/
to have something on, to be dressed in, to deteriorate		

She likes to **wear** her hair up when she's working.

She **wore** a white dress, which I found inappropriate at a funeral.

Frank has **worn** glasses for 40 years.

infinitive	past simple	past participle
withdraw /wɪð'drɔ:/	withdrew /wɪð'dru:/	withdrawn /wɪð'drɔ:n/

to take out, to retreat, to back away, to draw back, to pull out

America has **withdrawn** its troops from Iraq.

I **withdrew** some money from the ATM.

He had to **withdraw** from the elections due to health problems.

infinitive	past simple	past participle
write /raɪt/	wrote /rəʊt/	written /rɪtn/

to record, to take down, to compose

Have you ever **written** a poem?

Beethoven **wrote** nine complete symphonies.

Before starting to **write** your doctoral dissertation, you have to do a lot of research.

5. IRREGULAR VERBS TAKING THE SAME FORM IN PAST SIMPLE AND PAST PARTICIPLE

infinitive	past simple	past participle
abide /əˈbaɪd/	abode* /əˈbəʊd/ abided /əˈbaɪdɪd/	abode* /əˈbəʊd/ abided /əˈbaɪdɪd/
to tolerate, to bear, to live, to stay, to last, to carry on, to keep on		

** **abode** /əˈbəʊd/ - a form used in formal language in the sense of "to stay/live in a place". With other meanings **abided** /əˈbaɪdɪd/ is used.*

He was homeless all his life and **abided/abode** in an abandoned hut in the woods. (*old-fashioned*)

The old hermit **abided/abode** in a cave in the mountains.

Sara considered herself a model citizen who **abided** by the law at all times.

I can't **abide** people who harm or kill animals.

infinitive	past simple	past participle
alight /əˈlaɪt/	alighted /əˈlaɪtɪd/ alit* /əˈlɪt/ 🇬🇧	alighted /əˈlaɪtɪd/ alit* /əˈlɪt/ 🇬🇧
to get off, to disembark, to descend, to land		

** **alit** /əˈlɪt/ - a very rare past simple and past participle form used in British English.*

A blue dragonfly has **alighted** on a water lily on the pond. (*formal*)

She scattered bread crumbs and a flock of sparrows instantly **alighted** on the grass.

We **alighted** from the train at St Pancras Station.

Do not **alight** while the bus is still in motion.

infinitive	past simple	past participle
backslide /ˈbæk.slaɪd/	**backslid** /ˈbæk.slɪd/	**backslid** /ˈbæk.slɪd/ **backslidden** /ˈbæk.slɪdᵊn/
to relapse, to recidivate, to return to old bad habits		

He tried to go straight after leaving prison but quickly **backslid** after meeting his old gang.

Despite rehabilitation, she has recently **backslid/backslidden** again into abusing alcohol.

Liam had promised his wife to never cheat on her again but **backslid** after an attractive girl moved in next door.

infinitive	past simple	past participle
behold* /bɪˈhəʊld/	**beheld** /bɪˈheld/	**beheld** /bɪˈheld/
to see, to watch, to notice, to remark		

* *archaic/literary*

Theseus **beheld** the flames of the sacred grove and advanced therein.

Turning around, I **beheld** a tall woman dressed in black staring at me with a murderous look.

To look into the eyes of Charles Manson was to **behold** insanity.

infinitive	past simple	past participle
bend /bend/	**bent** /bent/	**bent** /bent/
to stoop, to hunch over, to buckle, to fold, to bow, to wind, to twist, to submit		

I hurt my arm and now cannot **bend** it.

He has **bent** so often to pick up litter that he now has a permanent stoop.

She **bent** and heard her knees crack.

infinitive	past simple	past participle
beseech* /bɪˈsiːtʃ/	**beseeched** /bɪˈsiːtʃəd/ **besought** /bɪˈsɔːt/	**beseeched** /bɪˈsiːtʃəd/ **besought** /bɪˈsɔːt/
to beg, to plead, to ask		

* *literary*

I **beseeched/besought** her to forgive me, but she wouldn't relent.

I've **beseeched/besought** him three times not to leave us.

If he doesn't get what he wants he **beseeches** one until he is blue in the face.

infinitive	past simple	past participle
bestrew* /bɪˈstruː/	bestrewed /bɪˈstruːd/	bestrewed /bɪˈstruːd/ bestrewn /bɪˈ struːn/

to sprinkle, to dust something with something, to cover something with scattered objects

* *literary*

Red poppies **bestrewed** the entire meadow.

Multicoloured rose petals were **bestrewn/bestrewed** all over the road to welcome and honour Her Majesty.

Though the walls of his mansion appear to be **bestrewed/bestrewn** with some of the world's most famous paintings, many, in fact, are simply copies.

infinitive	past simple	past participle
bind /baɪnd/	bound /baʊnd/	bound /baʊnd/

to rope, to link, to join, to unite, to oblige, to trim, to edge, to wail

Her hands were **bound** behind her back and her eyes covered with a blindfold.

These two tribes not only live at peace, but they are also strongly **bound** together by the same rituals and beliefs.

A bookbinder **binds** books.

infinitive	past simple	past participle
bleed /bliːd/	bled /bled/	bled /bled/

to lose blood, to ooze, to draw blood, to vent, to extort, to run (colour)

Her cut **bled** heavily for a long time.

He **bled** to death.

Tom is a plumber, so should know how to **bleed** radiators.

My new jeans **bled** during washing and are now very pale.

infinitive	past simple	past participle
breed /bri:d/	bred /bred/	bred /bred/
to rear, to reproduce, to raise, to cause, to bring up		

My grandmother **breeds** Jack Russell terriers to sell.

His actions have **bred** a potentially dangerous situation for everyone.

Mrs Taylor is a real countrywoman, born and **bred**. She would never live in the city.

infinitive	past simple	past participle
bring /brɪŋ/	brought /brɔ:t/	brought /brɔ:t/
to get, to fetch, to deliver, to import, to cause, to inflict, to introduce, to broadcast, to accompany, to escort, to induce		

Tell me what **brings** you here.

I've **brought** back the book I borrowed.

Her outlandish designs **brought** her great fame.

The new water park has **brought** many families to our city.

infinitive	past simple	past participle
build /bɪld/	built /bɪlt/	built /bɪlt/
to construct, to erect, to establish		

Nobody knows how the pyramids of Giza were actually **built**.

They've **built** an extension to their house.

The City Council is planning to **build** a new school.

infinitive	past simple	past participle
burn /bɜ:n/	burnt /bɜ:nt/ burned /bɜ:nd/	burnt /bɜ:nt/ burned /bɜ:nd/
to smoke, to flame, to fire, to set fire, to torch, to blaze, to ignite		

How did you **burn** your hand?

The entire building **burnt/burned** to the ground in the fire.
Oh, no! I've **burnt/burned** the dinner.

infinitive	past simple	past participle
buy /baɪ/	bought /bɔːt/	bought /bɔːt/
to purchase, to acquire, to believe, to bribe		

She's **bought** an expensive new car.
I initially **bought** his theory but it was later disproven by another scientist.
My mother doesn't **buy** fruit and vegetables at a supermarket.

infinitive	past simple	past participle
can /kæn/, /kən/	could /kʊd/, /kəd/	could /kʊd/, /kəd/
to be able to, to know how to		

A: **Can** you play chess? B: Yes, I **can**.
You **could** have warned me that you were coming.
I **could**n't do anything about it.

infinitive	past simple	past participle
catch /kætʃ/	caught /kɔːt/	caught /kɔːt/
to grab, to grasp, to capture, to trap, to snatch, to make it, to make out, to contract		

Is it still possible to **catch** the flu after being vaccinated?
We've just **caught** the last train to London.
The police **caught** a burglar last night.

infinitive	past simple	past participle
chide /tʃaɪd/	chided /tʃaɪdɪd/ chid* /tʃɪd/	chided /tʃaɪdɪd/ chid* /tʃɪd/ chidden* /ˈtʃɪdən/
to scold, to reprimand, to reprehend, to rebuke		

* *the past simple* ***chid*** */tʃɪ̱d/ and past participle* ***chid*** */tʃɪ̱d/*/***chidden*** */ˈtʃɪdᵊn/ forms are not widely used and not every dictionary includes them, so it is safer to use the form* ***chided*** */tʃaɪdɪd/.*

Anna is a permissive mother and never **chides** her children.

He **chided** me for being late.

I was **chided** for being rude to my teacher.

infinitive	past simple	past participle
cleave* /kli:v/	cleaved /kli:vd/ cleft /klɛft/ clove /kləʊv/	cleaved /kli:vd/ cleft /klɛft/ cloven /ˈkləʊvn/

to crack, to slit, to split, to adhere to, to be attached to, to be devoted to

* *the verb* ***cleave*** */kli:v/ in the sense of "to split/divide" takes the forms* ***cleaved/clove/cleft*** *in past simple and* ***cleaved/cloven/cleft*** *in past participle. With the meaning "to adhere to/to stick closely to" it takes the forms* ***cleaved*** *or* ***clove*** *in past simple and* ***cleaved*** *in past participle, e.g.*

He had **cleaved** to the coast road throughout his entire journey.

Sue **cleaved/clove** strongly to her faith, especially during times of adversity.

A single blow of the axe **cleaved/cleft/clove** the log in two.

infinitive	past simple	past participle
cling /klɪŋ/	clung /klʌŋ/	clung /klʌŋ/

to grab hold of something, to adhere, to fit closely, to stick to something

Young chimpanzees **cling** tightly to their mothers.

She's **clung** like a limpet to me when afraid.

He blindly **clung** to the hope that she would return.

infinitive	past simple	past participle
clothe /kləʊð/	clad /klæd/ clothed /kləʊðd/	clad /klæd/ clothed /kləʊðd/

to dress, to outfit, to attire

** when the verb **clothe** /kləʊð/ refers to the wearing of clothes, both **clothed** /kləʊðd/ and **clad** /klæd/ are correct. When we refer to a type of covering, especially one made of tougher material, such as that covering the outside of a building, the past simple and past participle of **clad** /klæd/ is preferred.*

We have six children to feed and **clothe**.

The queen was **clothed** in fine silks.

He was **clothed/clad** rather modestly for a king and oftentimes courtiers mistook him for a servant.

infinitive	past simple	past participle
creep /kriːp/	crept /krept/	crept /krept/
to crawl, to sneak, to skulk, to ramp, to stroke		

He must have **crept** in when I wasn't looking.

The burglar **crept** up the front door.

My niece likes to **creep** up behind people and shout 'Boo!' to frighten them.

Tim is always **creeping** to his boss.

infinitive	past simple	past participle
crossbreed /ˈkrɒs.briːd/	crossbred /ˈkrɒs.bred/	crossbred /ˈkrɒs.bred/
to hybridise, to cross-fertilize		

In the past, black-tailed jackrabbits were **crossbred** with snowshoe hares.

He has **crossbred** an apple and a pear to produce a fruit he calls a 'prapple'!

A crazy scientist plans to **crossbreed** a cat with a dog.

infinitive	past simple	past participle
crow /krəʊ/	crowed /krəʊd/ crew * /kruː/ 🇬🇧	crowed /krəʊd/
to squawk, to babble, to prattle		

** the past simple form **crew** /kruː/ of the verb **crow** /krəʊ/ occurs only in British English but the form **crowed** /krəʊd/ definitely prevails. In American English, the **crowed** /krəʊd/ form is used in past simple and past participle.*

The rooster has **crowed** three times.

The parents watched their baby **crow** with delight when they gave her a rattle.
After Peter's third denial of Jesus, the rooster **crowed/crew** a second time.

infinitive	past simple	past participle
daydream /ˈdeɪ.driːm/	daydreamt /ˈdeɪ.dremt/ daydreamed /ˈdeɪ.driːmd/	daydreamt /ˈdeɪ.dremt/ daydreamed /ˈdeɪ.driːmd/

to dream, to fantasise, to immerse in daydreams

Yesterday I **daydreamt/daydreamed** about being a famous singer.
She lay down on the grass and **daydreamed/daydreamt**.
He feels blissfully happy when he **daydreams** about living on a desert island.

infinitive	past simple	past participle
deal /diːl/	dealt /delt/	dealt /delt/

to trade, to commerce, to cooperate, to do business

He is known to **deal** in smuggled goods.
The manager **dealt** with the problem after a customer complained.
Oliver had **dealt** in cars for a living before setting up his own restaurant.

infinitive	past simple	past participle
dig /dɪg/	dug /dʌg/	dug /dʌg/

to burrow, to excavate, to mine, to understand, to like, to peek

He has just **dug** a deeper hole for himself by trying to explain his mistake.
The children **dug** a long tunnel in the snow.
Some dogs **dig** holes and hide bones in them.

infinitive	past simple	past participle
dive /daɪv/	dived /daɪvd/ dove /doʊv/	dived /daɪvd/

to plunge, to plummet, to submerge, to snorkel, to scuba-dive, to nose-dive

I've **dived** on the reef many times.

The pool isn't deep, so don't **dive** in head first.

The submersible **dived** to a depth of 10,000 feet.

infinitive	past simple	past participle
dream /dri:m/	dreamt /dremt/ 🇬🇧 dreamed /dri:md/ 🇺🇸 🇬🇧	dreamt /dremt/ 🇬🇧 dreamed /dri:md/ 🇺🇸 🇬🇧
to have a dream, to fantasise, to imagine		

What did you **dream** about last night?

Last night she **dreamt/dreamed** about being a princess.

He has **dreamt/dreamed** of being an astronaut since he was 8.

infinitive	past simple	past participle
dwell* /dwel/	dwelt /dwelt/ 🇬🇧 dwelled /dweld/ 🇺🇸 🇬🇧	dwelt /dwelt/ 🇬🇧 dwelled /dweld/ 🇺🇸 🇬🇧
to live, to reside, to stay		

* *formal/literary*

He **dwelt/dwelled** by a lake for twenty years.

The family had **dwelt/dwelled** in the wilderness since 1999.

I'm pretty sure that my parents won't let me go on a camp with the guys and **dwell** in a tent.

infinitive	past simple	past participle
feed /fi:d/	fed /fed/	fed /fed/
to give food, to nourish, to maintain, to graze, to fertilise, to input (data)		

Did you **feed** the fish?

I've **fed** the dog, so you don't need to give her any more food.

She **fed** her employers with lies, every one of which they believed.

infinitive	past simple	past participle
feel /fiːl/	felt /felt/	felt /felt/

to sense, to experience, to touch, to be under the impression, to believe, to figure

I just **felt** weird after taking the sleeping pill and couldn't drop off.
Can you **feel** the vein in my left arm?
I have **felt** the same way all along.

infinitive	past simple	past participle
fight /faɪt/	fought /fɔːt/	fought /fɔːt/

to battle, to scrap, to campaign, to combat, to contend, to argue

My grandfather **fought** in the Second World War.
They **fought** bravely but were eventually overrun by the enemy.
Whenever I go to visit them, they **fight**.

infinitive	past simple	past participle
find /faɪnd/	found /faʊnd/	found /faʊnd/

to discover, to detect, to retrieve, to come by, to encounter, to decide, to judge, to consider, to notice, to claim

I **find** his behaviour very peculiar.
I **found** my glasses! They were under the cushion.
The police **found** that Steve had been abused as a child.
I **found** my old photos in the attic.
He was **found** guilty of the charge.

infinitive	past simple	past participle
fit /fɪt/	fitted /ˈfɪtɪd/ 🇬🇧 fit /fɪt/ 🇺🇸	fitted /ˈfɪtɪd/ 🇬🇧 fit /fɪt/ 🇺🇸

to match, to suit, to mount, to install, to agree with, to adjust, to have a seizure

I don't think this table will **fit** into your small kitchen.

We've just had solar panels **fitted** to the roof of the house.

The High Court stated that the punishment had **fitted** the crime and so upheld the initial judgement.

infinitive	past simple	past participle
flee /fli:/	fled /fled/	fled /fled/
to escape, to run away		

He had **fled** Syria to be safe but found himself caught up in another war in Ukraine.

He **fled** abroad 15 years ago after being accused of murder.

My parents want to **flee** the city and live in the country.

infinitive	past simple	past participle
fling /flɪŋ/	flung /flʌŋ/	flung /flʌŋ/
to throw, to toss		

She **flung** her bag in the corner and sat down with a strong drink.

The window was **flung** open by the strong wind.

He **flings** himself into every activity with the same energy.

infinitive	past simple	past participle
foretell /fɔ:ˈtel/	foretold /fɔ:ˈtəʊld/	foretold /fɔ:ˈtəʊld/
to predict, to prophesy, to envisage, to tell fortunes		

He claimed to be the one who **foretold** the death of Kennedy.

The psychic has **foretold** that I will marry a prince.

No one can **foretell** the future.

infinitive	past simple	past participle
get* /get/	got /gɒt/	got /gɒt/ gotten** /ˈgɒt.ən/
to receive, to obtain, to buy, to bring, to convince, to persuade, to arrive, to reach, to earn, to prepare, to understand, to capture, to affect, to contract, to achieve		

* *the verb* ***get*** /get/ *has many different meanings and is used in many expressions.*

** *in American English, both* ***got*** *and* ***gotten*** *are used as past participles. The* ***got*** *form is used when the verb* ***get*** *means "to possess", "to have", while* ***gotten*** *is used only when the verb* ***get*** *means "to get/receive", "to become", or when it refers to some process or change, e.g.:*

British English:

- Petrol has ***got*** so expensive recently.
- I have ***got*** better at speaking English since I started a course.
- I've ***got*** an important matter to discuss with you.

American English:

- Petrol has ***gotten*** so expensive recently.
- I have ***gotten*** better at speaking English since I started a course.
- I've ***gotten*** some time off, am going camping.

Where did you **get** this coffee table?

I've **got** a strange rash on my leg.

Come here and have a look at what I've **got** for you.

Natasha **got** really angry with Sarah.

There was no bus, so we **got** a taxi.

infinitive	past simple	past participle
gild* /gɪld/	gilded /gɪldɪd/ gilt /gɪlt/	gilded /gɪldɪd/ gilt /gɪlt/
to cover or decorate with gold, to glisten		

* *literary*

The whole interior of the chamber was covered with gemstones and amber and the lanterns were **gilded/gilt** with red gold.

Looking at the rays of the setting sun as they **gilded/gilt** the smooth surface of the sea, she felt a sudden surge of new hope.

The craftsman decided not to **gild** the picture frame but leave it unadorned.

infinitive	past simple	past participle
grind /graɪnd/	ground /graʊnd/	ground /graʊnd/
to mince, to chop, to crush, to sharpen, gnash (the teeth), to jam		

The butcher **grinds** his knives twice a week.

My mum says that I **ground** my teeth while sleeping when I was young.

He has **ground** so many cigarette butts into the table that it's now permanently scarred.

Every morning he **ground** fresh coffee, savouring the aroma that filled the kitchen.

infinitive	past simple	past participle
hamstring /ˈhæmstrɪŋ/	hamstrung /ˈhæmstrʌŋ/	hamstrung /ˈhæmstrʌŋ/
to restrict, to limit, to obstruct, to make something difficult or impossible		

All production has been **hamstrung** by lack of labour.

The factory's business has been **hamstrung** due to the COVID-19 pandemic.

If he is elected the next president, he will **hamstring** our current trade embargo on Iran.

infinitive	past simple	past participle
hang /hæŋ/	hung /hʌŋ/ hanged* /hæŋd/	hung /hʌŋ/ hanged* /hæŋd/
to suspend, to dangle, to crash (computer), to hover, to spend time 🇺🇸		

** in situations where someone is killed by the act of hanging from a rope around their neck, only **hanged** /hæŋd/ is used. In other situations involving physical suspension, it is **hung** /hʌŋ/.*

We haven't **hung** the pictures yet.

He **hung** a string of pearls around her neck.

Can I **hang** my coat in the wardrobe?

They **hung** out together quite often.

He **hanged** himself.

infinitive	past simple	past participle
have /hæv/, /həv/	**had** /hæd/,/həd/	**had** /hæd/,/həd/
to own, to possess, to eat, to drink, to experience, to organise, to obtain, to receive		

The verb “**have**” has many different meanings.

They’ve **had** a lot of difficulties in their marriage.

We **had** a blissful childhood.

infinitive	past simple	past participle
hear /hɪər/	**heard** /hɜːd/	**heard** /hɜːd/
to listen, to catch, to find out, to learn		

I’ve **heard** that you’ve got engaged. Congratulations!

I can’t **hear** anything with such a noise.

She **heard** some steps behind the door.

I’ve **heard** a lot about her.

The jury would like to **hear** the witness now.

infinitive	past simple	past participle
hew /hjuː/	**hewed** /hjuːd/	**hewed** /hjuːd/ **hewn** /hjuːn/
to chip, to log, to hack, to axe		

Mount Rushmore was **hewn/hewed** in 10 %; the rest was carved using dynamite.

He **hewed** the statue out of sandstone.

Eleanor is the only woman who **hews** coal not worse than the other hewers.

Can you believe that this statue was entirely **hewed/hewn** out in wood?

infinitive	past simple	past participle
hold /həʊld/	**held** /held/	**held** /held/
to keep, to detain, to take place, to arrange, to store, to support, to consider, to accommodate		

The conference was **held** in the Seimas Palace.

Although I **held** the umbrella tightly in my hand, the wind managed to whip it away.

Could you **hold** my handbag for a moment?

Joseph has **held** the position of mayor for three terms.

infinitive	past simple	past participle
inlay /ˌɪnˈleɪ/	inlaid /ˌɪnˈleɪd/	inlaid /ˌɪnˈleɪd/
to decorate objects or surfaces with fine ornaments		

Small stones had been **inlaid** into the recesses of the pavement.

He used gold glitter to **inlay** a ceramic vase.

She **inlaid** rubies into the earrings.

infinitive	past simple	past participle
keep /kiːp/	kept /kept/	kept /kept/
to hold, to detain, to restrain, to remain, to prevent, to maintain, to continue, to store, to observe, to manage, to run, to respect		

When we lived on the farm, we **kept** cows, goats and sheep.

It's wise to **keep** all your tax returns.

Diana **kept** a diary nearly all her life.

Does your family **keep** the Sabbath?

infinitive	past simple	past participle
kneel /niːl/	knelt /nelt/ kneeled /niːld/	knelt /nelt/ kneeled /niːld/
to bow the knee, to get down on one's knees, to be on one's knees		

Dennis **knelt/kneeled** down on one knee and proposed to Dorothy.

She **knelt/kneeled** for the whole Mass.

Please stand up. There is no need to **kneel**.

infinitive	past simple	past participle
lay /leɪ/	laid /leɪd/	laid /leɪd/

to repose, to place, to put, to arrange, to put forward

Jenny likes to **lay** her make-up bag on the washbasin.

Why haven't you **laid** the table yet?

He **laid** his wedding ring on the table and left his wife without saying a word.

infinitive	past simple	past participle
lead /li:d/	led /led/	led /led/

to chair, to conduct, to guide, to link, to result in, to be in the lead

All roads **lead** to Rome.

Mr Roberts **led** the discussion.

Her behaviour has **led** me to believe that she can be trusted.

infinitive	past simple	past participle
lean /li:n/	leant /lent/ leaned /li:nd/	leant /lent/ leaned /li:nd/

to tilt, to stoop, to bend over, to incline

The pine **leant/leaned** over under the weight of the snow.

Lean your head back a little more.

She had previously **leant/leaned** towards socialism but now embraced conservatism.

infinitive	past simple	past participle
leap /li:p/	leapt /lept/ leaped /li:pt/	leapt /lept/ leaped /li:pt/

to jump, to vault, to hop

She had **leapt** over a puddle.

Do you want to **leap** over the fence?

My cat **leapt** up on the windowsill to look at the birds in the garden.

infinitive	past simple	past participle
learn /lɜːn/	learnt /lɜːnt/ 🇬🇧 learned /lɜːnd/ 🇺🇸 🇬🇧	learnt /lɜːnt/ 🇬🇧 learned /lɜːnd/ 🇺🇸 🇬🇧
to study, to acquire, to revise, to find out		

I've just **learnt/learned** that she's pregnant.
I have to **learn** this poem by heart by tomorrow.
He **learnt/learned** Spanish when he lived in Barcelona.

infinitive	past simple	past participle
leave /liːv/	left /left/	left /left/
to exit, to quit, to depart, to go away, to abandon, to forget, to resign		

She **left** her husband after 30 years of marriage.
The bus has just **left**.
Where can I **leave** my luggage?

infinitive	past simple	past participle
lend /lend/	lent /lent/	lent /lent/
to loan, to grant, to add		

When are you going to give me the money back that I **lent** you last month?
The bank won't **lend** me any money.
Your new hairstyle has **lent** you an air of gravity.

infinitive	past simple	past participle
light /laɪt/	lit /lɪt/ lighted* /ˈlaɪ.tɪd/	lit /lɪt/ lighted* /ˈlaɪ.tɪd/
to put on, to switch on, to brighten, to torch		

** the form **lighted** /ˈlaɪ.tɪd/ is also used in past simple and past participle, especially before nouns.*

They **lit/lighted** a fire on the beach.
He has **lit/lighted** his third cigar in the last hour.

Don't **light** the oil lamp in the barn! You could start a fire.
The bright lanterns **lit/lighted** the alleys in the park.

infinitive	past simple	past participle
lose /lu:z/	lost /lɒst/	lost /lɒst/

to mislay, to miss, to be defeated, to omit

Approximately 200 workers will **lose** their jobs if the company fails.
He has **lost** all his savings.
Your team **lost** 6-2.
Tragically, he **lost** both parents soon after he was born.

infinitive	past simple	past participle
make /meɪk/	made /meɪd/	made /meɪd/

to produce, to create, to perform, to cause, to force, to earn, to reach, to gain, to deliver, to appoint, to prepare, to amount to

She **makes** me happy.
I've **made** some tea for us.
George **made** a lot of money through writing e-books.

infinitive	past simple	past participle
mean /mi:n/	meant /ment/	meant /ment/

to say, to have in mind, to intend, to indicate, to be serious, to be important

What does this word **mean** in English?
I've **been meaning** to call you, but I was so busy.
This cutting-edge smart TV is **meant** to hang on the wall.
I **mean** it! Don't go there.
What I **meant** to tell her was that I love her.

infinitive	past simple	past participle
meet /mi:t/	met /met/	met /met/

to encounter, to get to know somebody, to come across, to fulfil, to settle

Regrettably, you did not **meet** all the necessary requirements.
He **met** his death in 1935 after a climbing accident.
I had **met** him before, but couldn't remember his name.

infinitive	past simple	past participle
misdeal /ˌmɪsˈdiːl/	misdealt /ˌmɪsˈdelt/	misdealt /ˌmɪsˈdelt/
to deal cards incorrectly		

You've **misdealt**. I've got only 10 cards.
Please shuffle and deal the cards again because I think they were **misdealt**.
Tim is so dishonest - he **misdeals** the cards every time we play.

infinitive	past simple	past participle
mishear /ˌmɪsˈhɪər/	misheard /ˌmɪsˈhɜːd/	misheard /ˌmɪsˈhɜːd/
to misunderstand what somebody says, to hear incorrectly		

I'm sure he didn't say that. You must have **misheard** him.
You **misheard** my name. It's Adam, not Allan.
She wouldn't have **misheard** if she had been paying attention.

infinitive	past simple	past participle
mislay* /ˌmɪsˈleɪ/	mislaid /ˌmɪsˈleɪd/	mislaid /ˌmɪsˈleɪd/
to lose, to misplace, to be unable to find something		

* *formal*

I must have **mislaid** the keys. They're not in my bag.
She **mislaid** her umbrella again.
Do you often **mislay** small things?

infinitive	past simple	past participle
mislead /ˌmɪsˈliːd/	misled /mɪs'led/	misled /mɪs'led/
to bluff, to misinform, to confuse someone by giving false information		

Sylvia wouldn't try to **mislead** you. It's not her way.

We think they've been deliberately **misled**.

He **misled** me into thinking he loved me.

infinitive	past simple	past participle
misspell /ˌmɪsˈspel/	misspelt /ˌmɪsˈspelt/ 🇬🇧 misspelled /ˌmɪsˈspeld/ 🇺🇸 🇬🇧	misspelt /ˌmɪsˈspelt/ 🇬🇧 misspelled /ˌmɪsˈspeld/ 🇺🇸 🇬🇧
to make a spelling mistake, to spell incorrectly		

You have **misspelt/misspelled** my second name.

I **misspelt/misspelled** my boss's surname.

Be careful with Latin words that you can easily **misspell**.

infinitive	past simple	past participle
misspend /ˌmɪsˈspend/	misspent /ˌmɪsˈspent/	misspent /ˌmɪsˈspent/
to waste, to squander		

A lot of public money was **misspent**.

He **misspent** all his money and now borrows from friends and family.

Don't **misspend** all your pocket money.

infinitive	past simple	past participle
misunderstand /ˌmɪs.ʌn.dəˈstænd/	misunderstood /mɪsʌndəˈstʊd/	misunderstood /mɪsʌndəˈstʊd/
to interpret something incorrectly, to take something the wrong way		

I think I've **misunderstood** her.

I told him to buy a gluten-free cake, but he **misunderstood** and bought a sugar-free cake.

He was **misunderstood** by most of us because his intentions were unclear.

infinitive	past simple	past participle
outfight /ˌaʊtˈfaɪt/	outfought /ˌaʊtˈ/fɔːt /	outfought /ˌaʊtˈ/fɔːt /
to fight better than somebody else, to defeat the opponent		

He wasn't considered a serious challenger, but in the last fight he **outfought** his opponent.

He's training hard to **outfight** his opponent.

The reigning champion was **outfought** by a 17-year-old boy in the ring.

infinitive	past simple	past participle
outleap /ˈaʊt.liːp/	outleapt /ˈaʊt.liːpt/ 🇬🇧 outleaped /ˈaʊt.liːpt/ 🇺🇸	outleapt /ˈaʊt.liːpt/ 🇬🇧 outleaped /ˈaʊt.liːpt/ 🇺🇸
to jump higher than somebody else		

The high jumper **outleapt** all competitors to claim a gold medal.

I've **outleapt** you by 2 centimetres.

To **outleap** your opponents and throw the ball to a team member is crucial in basketball.

infinitive	past simple	past participle
outsell /ˌaʊtˈsel/	outsold /ˌaʊtˈsəʊld/	outsold /ˌaʊtˈsəʊld/
to surpass in selling, to sell more goods that the competitor		

France habitually **outsells** Italy in the cheese market.

We have **outsold** our competitors on several occasions.

To get through a rough patch we offered more value on products and so **outsold** our competitors.

infinitive	past simple	past participle
outshine /ˌaʊtˈʃaɪn/	outshone /ˌaʊtˈʃɒn /	outshone /ˌaʊtˈʃɒn /
to overshadow, to surpass, to shine brighter than		

Although he is only 12, he **outshines** older pupils in maths.

Your daughter's performance **outshone** everyone else's in the play.

This supernova explosion has **outshone** all other explosions in the universe.

infinitive	past simple	past participle
overfeed /ˌəʊvəˈfiːd/	overfed /ˌəʊvəˈfed/	overfed /ˌəʊvəˈfed/
to eat or feed too much		

He **overfeeds** his cat - that's why it's so fat.

The baby was **overfed** and had to be taken to hospital.

My goldfish died because I had **overfed** them.

infinitive	past simple	past participle
overhang /ˌəʊ.vəˈhæŋ/	**overhung** /ˌəʊ.vəˈhʌŋ/	**overhung** /ˌəʊ.vəˈhʌŋ/
to hang over something, to extend over		

The route was shaded by trees which **overhung** the road.

Jason used to have a six-pack, but now his belly **overhangs** his belt.

Dense fog **overhung** the lake.

infinitive	past simple	past participle
overhear /ˌəʊ.vəˈhɪər/	**overheard** /ˌəʊ.vəˈhɜːd/	**overheard** /ˌəʊ.vəˈhɜːd/
to hear something unintentionally or by accident		

Excuse me Sir, I **overheard** you and I think you are totally wrong about the matter.

I've just **overheard** my parents saying they want to get a divorce.

Nevertheless, it's true. It doesn't matter that I **overheard** him.

infinitive	past simple	past participle
overlay /ˌəʊ.vəˈleɪ/	**overlaid** /ˌəʊ.vəˈleɪd/	**overlaid** /ˌəʊ.vəˈleɪd/
to cover, to coat, to enhance, to feature		

The Faberge egg was **overlaid** with a thin layer of gold and encrusted with precious stones.

In order to prevent the wood from deteriorating and make it resistant to weather it was **overlaid** with a thick layer of wood preservative.

The small comfort she gained from listening to classical music before take-off failed to **overlay** her fear of flying.

infinitive	past simple	past participle
overpay /ˌəʊ.vəˈpeɪ/	overpaid /ˌəʊ.vəˈpeɪd/	overpaid /ˌəʊ.vəˈpeɪd/
to pay too much, to make an excess payment		

I thought the phone bill was high and discovered that I had **overpaid** by £25.

The company managers were **overpaid,** whereas we worked for minimum wage.

The company tries not to **overpay** their employees for acquisition and will soon introduce a new tracking selling system.

infinitive	past simple	past participle
oversell /ˌəʊ.vəˈsel/	oversold /ˌəʊ.vəˈsold/	oversold /ˌəʊ.vəˈsold/
to sell too much or too many, to use aggressive methods in selling		

The concert tickets have been **oversold**.

Many airlines **oversell** flight tickets on the assumption that some passengers won't show up.

He always boasted and **oversold** his skills - he ended up working on a supermarket checkout.

infinitive	past simple	past participle
overshoot /ˌəʊ.vəˈʃuːt/	overshot /ˌəʊ.vəˈʃɒt /	overshot /ˌəʊ.vəˈʃɒt /
to get past, to miss, to omit, to overrun		

The Minister for Public Health has stated that he's seeking budget cuts in hospitals because they **overshot** last year.

The pilot had **overshot** the runway and landed in nearby grassland.

She tried to look trendy but **overshot** the mark and ended up looking silly.

infinitive	past simple	past participle
oversleep /ˌəʊ.vəˈsliːp/	overslept /ˌəʊ.vəˈslept/	overslept /ˌəʊ.vəˈslept/
to sleep too long		

I've **overslept** again.

She often **oversleeps** for work as she usually stays up very late.

He forgot to set up the alarm and **overslept**.

infinitive	past simple	past participle
overspend /ˌəʊ.vəˈspend/	overspent /ˌəʊ.vəˈspent/	overspent /ˌəʊ.vəˈspent/
to spend too much money		

He's **overspent** this month and now has to tighten his belt.

We definitely **overspent** last year.

If you **overspend** on holiday, you won't have enough left to buy presents.

infinitive	past simple	past participle
pay /peɪ/	paid /peɪd/	paid /peɪd/
to give money in return for services or goods, to settle a bill, to defray, to benefit		

Have you **paid** the electricity bill this month?

I **paid** only $50 for this suit.

It doesn't **pay** to dwell on the past.

infinitive	past simple	past participle
plead /pli:d/	pleaded /pli:dɪd/ pled /pled/	pleaded /pli:dɪd/ pled /pled/
to request, to beg, to appeal, to claim, to defend, to justify		

My sister **pleaded** with me to babysit her children for at least one evening.

He had **pleaded** innocent to the crime but the judge found him guilty.

A beggar on the street **pleaded** with me to give him some change.

infinitive	past simple	past participle
prepay /ˌpri:ˈpeɪ/	prepaid /ˌpri:ˈpeɪd/	prepaid /ˌpri:ˈpeɪd/
to pay in advance		

I've **prepaid** 10 % of the phone's value to get it on contract.

The shipment fees are **prepaid**.

infinitive	past simple	past participle
prove /pruːv/	proved /pruːvd/	proved /pruːvd/ proven /pruːvn/
to demonstrate that, to verify, to determine, to turn out		

How are you going to **prove** him wrong?
She has **proved** her innocence and has been set free.
The exam **proved** to be exceptionally difficult.

infinitive	past simple	past participle
rebuild /ˌriːˈbɪld/	rebuilt /ˌriːˈbɪlt/	rebuilt /ˌriːˈbɪlt/
to restore, to reconstruct, to recreate, to renovate		

The castle was destroyed during the war and **rebuilt** 20 years later.
The church has been **rebuilt** and is even more beautiful than previously.
We're planning to **rebuild** our house this year.

infinitive	past simple	past participle
relay /ˌrɪˈleɪ/	relaid /ˌrɪˈleɪd/ relayed* /ˌrɪˈleɪd/	relaid /ˌrɪˈleɪd/ relayed* /ˌrɪˈleɪd/
to broadcast, to transmit, to pass on, to lay again		

** the verb **relay** /ˌrɪˈleɪ/ also has a past simple and a past participle form: **relayed** /ˌrɪˈleɪd/, where **relay** means "to retransmit", "to broadcast" (e.g. a TV programme), "to pass on" (e.g. a message, news), "to change" (e.g. someone at work during the shift), e.g. She immediately **relayed** the news to everybody.*

The paving stones will have to be **relaid**.
She **relaid** the carpet in the bedroom because it needed some adjustment.
He was concerned that his information be **relayed** to the right authorities.
She **relayed** the news to everybody as soon as she returned home.

infinitive	past simple	past participle
remake /ˌriːˈmeɪk/	remade /ˌriːˈmeɪd/	remade /ˌriːˈmeɪd/

to make something again or differently (film, song, book), to record again, to reshoot, to alter, to redo

How many times has the film "Robin Hood" been **remade**?

She **remade** her wedding dress into an evening gown.

Susan always **remakes** the bed after a nap.

infinitive	past simple	past participle
rend* /rend/	rent /rent/ rended /rendɪd/	rent /rent/ rended /rendɪd/

to tear, to rip, to rive, to cause emotional pain

* *archaic/literary*

He sank to his knees, **rent** his garments and yelled hopelessly in a language that nobody could understand.

His heart was **rent** by the knowledge that his wife was cheating on him.

It was the practice of the newly-widowed, distraught with grief, to **rend** their hair in public.

infinitive	past simple	past participle
repay /rɪˈpeɪ/	repaid /rɪˈpeɪd/	repaid /rɪˈpeɪd/

to return (money), to pay back, to return a favour, to pay off

It wasn't easy to **repay** all the debts in such a short time.

I've **repaid** the money I owe.

The investment was quite risky, but it **repaid**.

infinitive	past simple	past participle
resell /ˌriːˈsel/	resold /ˌriːˈsəʊld/	resold /ˌriːˈsəʊld/

to sell back, to sell something again

He **resold** his new car after using it only for six months.

Dan buys up old furniture, refurbishes it, and **resells** it.

The shop fixed the old bike and then **resold** it for three times the purchase price.

infinitive	past simple	past participle
resit /ˌriːˈsɪt/	resat /ˌriːˈsæt/	resat /ˌriːˈsæt/
to retake an exam		

He failed the exam and **resat** it the following term.

Maria has **resat** the French examination twice but still failed to pass.

You can only **resit** this test twice.

infinitive	past simple	past participle
retell /ˌriːˈtel/	retold /ˌriːˈtəʊld /	retold /ˌriːˈtəʊld /
to tell (a story, a joke) again		

My grandmother has **retold** this story many times.

I **retold** a joke she had already heard.

I had to **retell** my story to more than one police officer.

infinitive	past simple	past participle
rethink /ˌriːˈθɪŋk/	rethought /ˌriːˈθɔːt/	rethought /ˌriːˈθɔːt/
to reconsider, to have a think		

Ok, I'll **rethink** the problem and let you know.

He had **rethought** his attitude and decided to apologise.

Alec **rethought** the entire process and finally realised where he had gone wrong.

infinitive	past simple	past participle
rewind /ˌriːˈwaɪnd/	rewound /ˌriːˈwaʊnd/	rewound /ˌriːˈwaʊnd/
to reverse, to wind (a film/tape) to the beginning		

The policeman **rewound** the video tape and spotted something suspicious.

We **rewound** the tape to replay a passage about the man who robs the local shops.

Rachel wanted to **rewind** the message on the answering machine and listen to it once more but she accidentally erased it.

infinitive	past simple	past participle
say /seɪ/	said /sed/	said /sed/

to tell, to express, to speak, to state

What did he **say**?

He **said** that he wouldn't be coming to the party.

I didn't have my glasses so couldn't see what the clock actually **said.**

infinitive	past simple	past participle
seek* /siːk/	sought /sɔːt/	sought /sɔːt/

to look for, to search for, to pursue

* *formal*

She **sought** justice but was unable to find any.

We **seek** perfection to compensate for our sense of inadequacy.

You should have **sought** legal advice before you took any action.

infinitive	past simple	past participle
sell /sel/	sold /səʊld/	sold /səʊld/

to trade, to deal in, to be for sale, to persuade

She wants to **sell** all her unused clothes online.

My brother-in-law **sold** me on the idea that portfolio investment was profitable.

I'm sorry, I've just **sold** the last piece.

infinitive	past simple	past participle
send /send/	sent /sent/	sent /sent/

to post, to mail, to dispatch, to ship

We've **sent** you all the details.

I **sent** him an email yesterday.

I'm going to **send** a bunch of roses to my wife at work.

infinitive	past simple	past participle
shear /ʃɪər/	sheared /ʃɪəd/	sheared /ʃɪəd/ shorn /ʃɔːn/
to trim, to cut, to shave		

The farmer **sheared** over 50 sheep an hour.

The barber has **sheared/shorn** my hair and trimmed my beard.

Jenny **sheared** all her hair off and was almost unrecognisable.

infinitive	past simple	past participle
shine /ʃaɪn/	shone /ʃɒn/	shone /ʃɒn/
to glow, to gleam, to glitter, to polish		

Dewdrops on the grass **shone** in the morning sunlight.

Sam **shines** his motorbike after washing it.

His shoes **shone** brightly after being polished.

infinitive	past simple	past participle
shoe /ʃuː/	shod /ʃɒd/	shod /ʃɒd/
to fix a hoof with a horseshoe		

I've **shod** horses all my life - I know what I'm doing.

The invention of metal in the 1st century BC gave rise to the creation of metal sandals called solea ferrea, which were also used to **shoe** horses' hooves.

The blacksmith **shod** my horses last week.

infinitive	past simple	past participle
shoot /ʃuːt/	shot /ʃɒt/	shot /ʃɒt/
to gun down, to fire, to hunt, to speed, to film		

"The Lord of the Rings" trilogy was **shot** entirely in New Zealand.

He has **shot** into the lead in the race. But will he win?

My Uncle Ben used to **shoot** game.

infinitive	past simple	past participle
sit /sɪt/	**sat** /sæt/	**sat** /sæt/
to be seated, to take a seat, to seat, to place, to put, to be located, to babysit		

I've **sat** your little statue of Buddha in the garden.
The castle **sat** on a high mountain.
She doesn't want to **sit** the exam because she is afraid of failing it.

infinitive	past simple	past participle
sleep /sli:p/	**slept** /slept/	**slept** /slept/
to go to bed and rest, to go to sleep, to be asleep		

He's **slept** only two hours.
New York is the city that apparently never **sleeps**.
Yesterday, I **slept** all day.

infinitive	past simple	past participle
slide /slaɪd/	**slid** /slɪd/	**slid** /slɪd/
to glide, to slip, to slither, to slump, to slip out, to drop, to worsen		

She **slid** on the frozen lake.
Those rocks had **slid** down the mountain even before the earthquake.
Some experts predict that the global economy will **slide** next year.

infinitive	past simple	past participle
sling /slɪŋ/	**slung** /slʌŋ/	**slung** /slʌŋ/
to throw, to cast, to fling, to chuck, to hang		

She **slung** her coat on a peg and went to the living room.
I was **slung** out of the school for drinking alcohol.
Don't just **sling** your shoes on the carpet!

infinitive	past simple	past participle
slink /slɪŋk/	slunk /slʌŋk/	slunk /slʌŋk/

to creep, to draw away, to sneak

She has just **slunk** off without saying goodbye.

The boys **slunk** out of the house and went to the park.

It was ironic to see a comedian **slink** away in embarrassment after the audience didn't find his performance amusing.

infinitive	past simple	past participle
smell /smel/	smelt /smelt/ smelled /smeld/	smelt /smelt/ smelled /smeld/

to sniff, to have a smell of something, to stink, to scent

Do you **smell** something burning?

The cake **smelt/smelled** really good and tasted even better.

I've just **smelt/smelled** the fish you bought and it's definitely off!

infinitive	past simple	past participle
sneak /sni:k/	sneaked /sni:kt/ snuck* /snʌk/	sneaked /sni:kt/ snuck* /snʌk/

to steal, to smuggle, to snitch, to swipe

* *the form* ***snuck*** */snʌk/ is often used colloquially in American English and increasingly in British English.*

The cat **sneaked** up on the mouse and pounced on it.

A: Where's Martin? B: He's just **sneaked** out.

They want to **sneak** some beer into the school party.

infinitive	past simple	past participle
speed /spi:d/	speeded /ˈspi:dɪd/ sped /sped/	speeded /ˈspi:dɪd/ sped /sped/

*to accelerate, to rush, to race, to exceed the speed limit**

****speed** /spi:d/ in the sense of "exceeding the speed limit" is used in continuous tenses.*

There's no need to **speed**. We have two hours to get there.
A drunk driver has **sped** down the road and crashed into a lamppost.
He **sped** along the road in his new car.

infinitive	past simple	past participle
spell /spel/	spelt /spelt/ spelled /speld/	spelt /spelt/ spelled /speld/

to pronounce or write a word letter by letter, to herald

Could you **spell** your name for me, please?
Many English words were **spelt/spelled** differently in the past.
The dark clouds **spelt/spelled** rain.

infinitive	past simple	past participle
spend /spend/	spent /spent/	spent /spent/

to expend, to pay out, to hang, to consume, to use up

Mark's irresponsible. He's just **spent** all his monthly salary on computer games.
Where are you planning to **spend** your holiday this summer?
She **spent** a lot of time and energy planning her revenge.

infinitive	past simple	past participle
spit /spɪt/	spat /spæt/ spit /spɪt/	spat /spæt/ spit /spɪt/

to flob, to gob, to expectorate, to eject, to drizzle

That woman has just **spat** at that man.
He **spat** the food out because it tasted horrible.
Come on! **Spit** it out. I want to know the truth.

infinitive	past simple	past participle
spill /spɪl/	spilt /spɪlt/ spilled /spɪld/	spilt /spɪlt/ spilled /spɪld/
slop, pour, overflow, scatter		

She's just **spilt/spilled** coffee on my new carpet!

Please don't **spill** my drink.

When the concert was over, people **spilt/spilled** out of the amphitheatre into the surrounding streets.

infinitive	past simple	past participle
spin /spɪn/	spun /spʌn/	spun /spʌn/ span*/spæn/
to circle, to whirl, to swirl, to rotate, to yarn, to scoot, to tell		

* *the form* ***span*** */spæn/ as past participle is also used in British English.*

The spider has **spun/span** a web.

The washing machine **spun** for a few minutes and then broke down.

Spin the wheel of fortune and see what lies in store for you.

infinitive	past simple	past participle
spoil /spɔɪl/	spoilt /spɔɪlt/ spoiled /spɔɪld/	spoilt /spɔɪlt/ spoiled /spɔɪld/
to destroy, to ruin, to waste, to pamper, to indulge		

We should have eaten those cherries before. Now they've **spoilt/spoiled**.

My mother loves to **spoil** my daughter.

Sharron completely **spoilt/spoiled** my birthday party by getting drunk.

infinitive	past simple	past participle
stand /stænd/	stood /stʊd/	stood /stʊd/
to be on one's feet, to put up with, to tolerate, to be located, to place, to resist, to be in force		

I can't **stand** his arrogance.

We **stood** in the rain for 20 minutes.

That statue had **stood** for centuries before it was destroyed.

infinitive	past simple	past participle
stick /stɪk/	stuck /stʌk/	stuck /stʌk/
to glue, to paste, to tuck, to attach, to adhere		

We can try to **stick** this torn photograph together with tape.

We were **stuck** in traffic for two hours.

A little boy **stuck** his tongue out to me.

infinitive	past simple	past participle
strike /straɪk/	struck /strʌk/	struck /strʌk/
to hit, to stab, to go on strike, to knock, to beat		

The miners are threatening to **strike** if they don't get a pay rise.

He was **struck** by lightning and died instantly.

The prisoner **struck** a prison officer before being wrestled to the ground.

infinitive	past simple	past participle
string /strɪŋ/	strung /strʌŋ/	strung /strʌŋ/
to thread, to hang up, to tighten		

I **strung** Christmas lights up in my bedroom.

He's finally **strung** the guitar and will now play for us.

String the mushrooms on a thread and place them in sunlight to dry.

infinitive	past simple	past participle
sweat /swet/	sweated /ˈswetɪd/ sweat* /swet/	sweated /ˈswetɪd/ sweat* /swet/
to perspire, to drudge, to slave, to worry, to exploit, to bleed, to repent		

* *it is customary to use the form* **sweat** */swet/ as a past simple and past participle form when the verb* **sweat** */swet/ means "to exude unpleasantly-smelled liquid*

through the pores of the skin". In other senses, the form **sweated** */ˈswetɪd/ is used.*

I've never **sweat** so much in my entire life.

The room had no air-conditioning and we **sweat** all night.

He **sweated** like a pig at the gym.

infinitive	past simple	past participle
sting /stɪŋ/	stung /stʌŋ/	stung /stʌŋ/
to bite (a wasp), to burn, to prick, to provoke		

My eyes **stung** after I got soap in them while washing my face.

Ouch! A bee has just **stung** me.

She's very sharp and her words can **sting** sometimes.

infinitive	past simple	past participle
sweep /swiːp/	swept /swept/	swept /swept/
to brush, to clean, to glide, to rocket, to spread		

Take the broom and **sweep** all the corridors.

The tide was so strong that it **swept** the yacht out to sea.

The pandemic has **swept** the whole of the country.

infinitive	past simple	past participle
swing /swɪŋ/	swung /swʌŋ/	swung /swʌŋ/
to rock, to sway, to wave, to brandish, to turn back, to change, to haul off		

Her mood frequently **swings** from elation to depression.

The children **swung** on a rope over the river.

I've **swung** it! I've arranged for you to be promoted to Senior Manager.

infinitive	past simple	past participle
teach /tiːtʃ/	taught /tɔːt/	taught /tɔːt/
to instruct, to coach, to train, to school, to give lessons		

He might have graduated from university as a teacher, but he doesn't know how to **teach** properly.

I was **taught** to swim when I was 4.

Being fired has **taught** me a valuable life lesson: don't argue with your boss.

infinitive	past simple	past participle
tell /tel/	told /təʊld/	told /təʊld/
to say, to talk, to inform, to order, to distinguish, to see		

I've already **told** her not to do it again. It's best if you don't say anything more.

Many students can't **tell** the difference between the Present Perfect and Past Simple tense when they first start learning English.

He **told** them not to buy him any presents for his birthday this year.

infinitive	past simple	past participle
think /θɪŋk/	thought /θɔ:t/	thought /θɔ:t/
to conceive, to ponder, to believe, to consider, to assume		

What do you **think** of my fiancé?

I **thought** you wouldn't take the joke so seriously.

I've **thought** about this for a long time and decided not to do it.

infinitive	past simple	past participle
unbend /ˌʌnˈbend/	unbent /ˌʌnˈbent/	unbent /ˌʌnˈbent/
to relax, to chill out, to straighten		

True, she has **unbent** a little but she's still quite reserved.

Unbend the spring and place it between the metal inserts.

When he **unbent** and straightened up we could see how incredibly tall he was.

infinitive	past simple	past participle
unbind /ʌnˈbaɪnd/	unbound /ʌnˈbaʊn.d/	unbound /ʌnˈbaʊn.d/
to unfasten, to untie, to undo, to free, to release		

She had **unbound** her hair in an attempt to seduce him.

My captor refused to **unbind** me even when I went to the toilet.

It was a daredevil stunt, but somehow, he **unbound** the rope wrapped around his wrists and managed to escape from the tank filled with water.

infinitive	past simple	past participle
underpay /ˌʌndəˈpeɪ/	underpaid /ˌʌndəˈpeɪd/	underpaid /ˌʌndəˈpeɪd/
to pay less or not enough		

I quit the job because I was **underpaid**.

The regulation allows the employer to overpay some workers and **underpay** others.

Teachers are overworked and **underpaid**.

infinitive	past simple	past participle
undersell /ˌʌndəˈsel/	undersold /ˌʌndəˈsəʊld/	undersold /ˌʌndəˈsəʊld/
to sell goods cheaper than a competitor, to diminish oneself		

You didn't get the job because you **undersold** your skills at the interview.

The supermarket had **undersold** staple products like bread, which eventually forced some local shops to close.

Don't **undersell** yourself if you want to get a promotion.

infinitive	past simple	past participle
understand /ˌʌndəˈstænd/	understood /ˌʌndəˈstʊd/	understood /ˌʌndəˈstʊd/
to comprehend, to grasp, to believe		

Magda does not **understand** the seriousness of the whole situation.

Yes, I've **understood** everything you told me.

She **understood** from the nuns that life in the convent would make her a better person.

infinitive	past simple	past participle
unmake /ʌnˈmeɪk/	unmade /ʌnˈmeɪd/	unmade /ʌnˈmeɪd/
to cancel, to call off, to remove, to destroy		

This ridiculous law should be **unmade** immediately.

His lifelong reputation was **unmade** in minutes after the announcement.

The judge ruled that the current law did not serve the people and should be **unmade** immediately.

infinitive	past simple	past participle
unsay /ʌnˈseɪ/	**unsaid** /ʌnˈsed/	**unsaid** /ʌnˈsed/
to call off, to take back what was said		

Everybody knows you chose to leave it **unsaid**.

What is said cannot be **unsaid**.

If you **unsay** this, I will have no respect towards you.

infinitive	past simple	past participle
unwind /ˌʌnˈwaɪnd/	**unwound** /ˌʌnˈwaʊnd/	**unwound** /ˌʌnˈwaʊnd/
to relax, to calm down, to unwrap, to undo, to untwist		

When the doctor **unwound** the bandage, the injury appeared to have healed.

A glass of herbal tea always helps **unwind** me at the end of the day.

She has **unwound** the scarf from around her neck.

Sitting in the garden and listening to the blackbirds was the only thing that truly **unwound** her after a stressful day.

infinitive	past simple	past participle
uphold /ʌpˈhəʊld/	**upheld** /ʌpˈheld/	**upheld** /ʌpˈheld/
to maintain, to stand by, to sustain, to retain in force		

My final decision is that I **uphold** Mr Green's complaint.

Judge Moore **upheld** the lower court's decision.

Her claim for compensation for moral harm was **upheld**.

infinitive	past simple	past participle
waylay /weɪˈleɪ/	**waylaid** /weɪˈleɪd/	**waylaid** /weɪˈleɪd/
to ambush, to attack, to block somebody's way, to stop		

Sorry I'm late, but I was **waylaid** by the boss.

He was **waylaid** on the road to London by Dick Turpin and robbed of all he had.

Mrs Wrigley is a huge gossip. Every morning when I leave for work she **waylays** me with the latest news about our neighbours.

infinitive	past simple	past participle
weep /wi:p/	wept /wept/	wept /wept/
to cry, to sob, to ooze		

He almost **wept** with joy when she announced that she was expecting his child.

A thick yellow fluid **wept** from the wound after he scratched the scab off.

Each time I ask for an explanation, she **weeps** crocodile tears.

infinitive	past simple	past participle
win /wɪn/	won /wʌn/	won /wʌn/
to succeed, to come first, to gain, to earn		

You've **won**. I give up.

How can one **win** his respect?

They **won** the jackpot in the lottery.

infinitive	past simple	past participle
wind /waɪnd/ wind* /wɪnd/	wound /waʊnd/ winded* /wɪndɪd/	wound /waʊnd/ winded* /wɪndɪd/
to wrap, to loop, to coil, to regulate (clock)		

** the verb **wind** /wɪnd/ also has the irregular form **winded** /wɪndɪd/ (past simple and past participle), where it means "to make someone unable to breathe" or "to gently tap a baby's back to make it burp", e.g.*

His opponent's blow **winded** him and he lay unconscious for 10 minutes.

She **winded** the baby after feeding it to make it easier to burp.

I've **wound** (up) my watch but it still won't work.

The path **winds** through the woods to the river.

Her knee hurt so she **wound** a bandage around it.

infinitive	past simple	past participle
withhold* /wɪð'həʊld/	withheld /wɪð'held/	withheld /wɪð'held/
to keep secret, to hold back, to hide, to arrest, to refrain		

* *formal*

The government decided to **withhold** her new passport after it emerged she was using someone else's name.

The witness has **withheld** his testimony.

His salary was **withheld** after they suspected him of embezzlement.

infinitive	past simple	past participle
withstand* /wɪð'stænd/	withstood /wɪð'stʊd/	withstood /wɪð'stʊd/
to last, to resist, to stand up		

* *formal*

This high-rise building was designed in such a way as to **withstand** an earthquake.

His works have **withstood** the test of time.

The doctor said that it was a miracle she **withstood** such intense cold without freezing to death.

infinitive	past simple	past participle
wring /rɪŋ/	wrung /rʌŋ/	wrung /rʌŋ/
to mangle, to squeeze, to coerce		

She **wrung** the washing and hung it out to dry in the sun.

The mafia had **wrung** a huge amount of protection money out of the owner of the casino.

I'll **wring** your neck when I get a hold of you!

6. IRREGULAR VERBS WITH THE SAME FORM IN THE INFINITIVE, PAST SIMPLE AND AS PAST PARTICIPLE

infinitive	past simple	past participle
beset* /bɪˈset/	beset /bɪˈset/	beset /bɪˈset/
to trouble, to harass, to keep after somebody, to hem in		

* *formal*

My employer still hasn't paid me for overtime, explaining that the company is **beset** with financial difficulties.

Money problems have **beset** the company lately.

Retraining in a useful skill was a problem that **beset** the majority of the unemployed.

infinitive	past simple	past participle
bet /bet/	bet /bet/	bet /bet/
to wager, to gamble, to imagine		

He **bet** €10.000 on a horse that came last.

I **bet** she can't do it.

She **bet** me all her wage that I wouldn't do a bungee jump.

infinitive	past simple	past participle
bid /bɪd/	bid /bɪd/	bid /bɪd/
to offer, to extend an offer, to declare		

Have you really **bid** 1 million dollars for that painting?

You can **bid** for the items online in this auction.

Many contestants on the TV programme **bid** to become the top chef, but there can only ever be one winner.

infinitive	past simple	past participle
broadcast /ˈbrɔːdkɑːst/	broadcast /ˈbrɔːdkɑːst/ broadcasted /ˈbrɔːdkɑːstɪd/	broadcast /ˈbrɔːdkɑːst/ broadcasted /ˈbrɔːdkɑːstɪd/

to air, to transmit, to stream, to announce

The performance was **broadcast** live all over Europe.

Next weekend they will **broadcast** the president's speech.

He **broadcasts** every rumour and item of gossip he hears.

infinitive	past simple	past participle
burst /bɜːst/	burst /bɜːst/	burst /bɜːst/

to crack, to explode, to blow up, to be keen to do something

Her wardrobe was **bursting** with new clothes that it was unlikely she would ever wear – not that it stopped her, buying more new clothes.

He **burst** into laughter and couldn't say a word.

The water pipe might **burst** if the temperature drops below zero.

infinitive	past simple	past participle
bust* /bʌst/	bust /bʌst/ busted /ˈbʌstɪd/	bust /bʌst/ busted /ˈbʌstɪd/

to break, to smash, to catch, to arrest, to downgrade

** the verb **bust** /bʌst/ is an informal verb, considered a colloquialism in both British and American English. According to Longman Dictionary, the past simple and past participle forms are **bust** /bʌst/ or **busted** /ˈbʌstɪd/, with **bust** preferred in British English and **busted** in American English.*

*The following examples of sentences with the form **bust/busted** would not likely be used by a British English speaker, unless they were heavily influenced by Americanisms or were unaware of the correct use of British English.*

I **bust** my phone while rushing to work this morning. (*informal*)

I **smashed/broke** my phone while rushing to work this morning.

My brother-in-law was **busted** for possession of drugs. (*informal*)

My brother-in-law was **arrested** for possession of drugs. 🇬🇧

She **busted** her family-run café by taking a lot of payday loans. (*informal*) 🇺🇸
Her family-run café **went bankrupt** due to a lot of payday loans she took. 🇬🇧

*Moreover, in American English the past simple and past participle of the verb **bust** is "**bust**" in the sense of smash/break/go bankrupt, and "**busted**" in the sense of arrest or demote, for example:*

I have just **bust** my head against the wall. 🇺🇸
I have just **smashed/hit** my head against the wall. 🇬🇧

Ryan was **busted** to a private as punishment for a misdemeanour. 🇺🇸
Ryan was **downgraded/demoted** to a private as punishment for a misdemeanour. 🇬🇧

infinitive	past simple	past participle
cast /kɑːst/	cast /kɑːst/	cast /kɑːst/
to throw a shadow, to mould, to select (actors), to bestow, to throw off		

The director had **cast** her in the leading role, though the producer wasn't convinced of his choice.
The kerosene lamp **cast** a dark shadow on the walls of the empty room.
How do you **cast** a face in plaster?

infinitive	past simple	past participle
cost /kɒst/	cost /kɒst/ costed* /ˈkɒstɪd/	cost /kɒst/ costed* /ˈkɒstɪd/
to sell at, to have a price, to estimate the value of something		

** the verb **cost** /kɒst/ also has the past simple form and the past participle **costed** /ˈkɒstɪd/, where it means "to estimate the cost", e.g. He'd **costed** the entire investment and decided that it was unprofitable.*

My new iPhone **cost** a lot.
A: How much did it **cost**? B: €30.
That faulty electric toaster nearly **cost** me my life.

infinitive	past simple	past participle
cut /kʌt/	cut /kʌt/	cut /kʌt/

to slice, to chop, to slash, to wound, to reduce, to carve

Ow! I've **cut** my finger.

Cut the pizza into six pieces.

The company would not have survived if it hadn't drastically **cut** the price of its products.

infinitive	past simple	past participle
forecast /ˈfɔːkɑːst/	forecast /ˈfɔːkɑːst/ forecasted /ˈfɔːkɑːstɪd/	forecast /ˈfɔːkɑːst/ forecasted /ˈfɔːkɑːstɪd/

to predict, to foretell

Heavy rainfall has been **forecast/forecasted** for today on the East Coast.

Many believe that Nostradamus **forecast/forecasted** the outbreak of the coronavirus pandemic.

I took my umbrella as heavy rain was **forecast/forecasted** today, but it turned out to be very sunny.

infinitive	past simple	past participle
hit /hɪt/	hit /hɪt/	hit /hɪt/

to strike, to punch, to run into, to affect, to reach, to gain

The current unemployment situation is likely to **hit** us as well.

He lost control of the car and **hit** the fence.

Terrorists **hit** the World Trade Centre in 2001.

infinitive	past simple	past participle
hurt /hɜːt/	hurt /hɜːt/	hurt /hɜːt/

to injure, to ache, to harm, to damage

Your words have **hurt** her deeply. You need to apologise.

Did it **hurt** much?

You are only **hurting** yourself - no one else.

infinitive	past simple	past participle
input /ˈɪnpʊt/	input /ˈɪnpʊt/ inputted /ˈɪnpʊtɪd/	input /ˈɪnpʊt/ inputted /ˈɪnpʊtɪd/
to enter (data)		

Have you **input/inputted** all the data into the system yet?

She **input/inputted** all the monthly expenditures to the spreadsheet.

As a data administrator, your main responsibility is to **input** all data to our database.

infinitive	past simple	past participle
knit /nɪt/	knit* /nɪt/ knitted /ˈnɪtɪd/	knit* /nɪt/ knitted /ˈnɪtɪd/
to unite, to grow together, to heal (bone), to make clothes with knitting needles		

* *the form* ***knit*** */nɪt/ as past simple and past participle is used in the sense of to join somebody/something together, or to make a broken bone grow again. In the sense of making clothes with knitting needles, the form* ***knit*** */nɪt/ or* ***knitted*** */ˈnɪtɪd/ can be used.*

She has **knitted/knit** this pattern many times before.

The bone of his broken wrist **knit** together very quickly.

They are **knit** together by a common cultural background.

infinitive	past simple	past participle
let /let/	let /let/	let /let/
to allow, to permit, to lease		

I don't **let** my children go to bed late.

The flat is already **let**.

If you had **let** me help you, you wouldn't be in such a difficult situation now.

infinitive	past simple	past participle
lip-read /ˈlɪp riːd/	lip-read /ˈlɪp red/	lip-read /ˈlɪp red/
to understand speech from lip movements		

My aunt teaches deaf children to **lip-read**.

She lost her hearing at the age of 8, but only a few months later she could **lip-read** easily.

Learning to **lip-read** is challenging as many enunciation patterns resemble others.

infinitive	past simple	past participle
miscast /ˌmɪsˈkɑːst/	**miscast** /ˌmɪsˈkɑːst/	**miscast** /ˌmɪsˈkɑːst/
to assign an unsuitable role to an actor		

The director has definitely **miscast** the lead role, but no one can convince him otherwise.

I think Tom Cruise was **miscast** in "War of the Worlds".

To **miscast** an actor or actress can ruin a film.

infinitive	past simple	past participle
mishit /ˌmɪsˈhɪt/	**mishit** /ˌmɪsˈhɪt/	**mishit** /ˌmɪsˈhɪt/
to miss, to overshoot		

Emmanuel Emenike has again **mishit** his shot.

He had a couple of good opportunities, but sadly **mishit** both times.

How could you **mishit** so badly?

infinitive	past simple	past participle
misread /ˌmɪsˈriːd/	**misread** /ˌmɪsˈred/	**misread** /ˌmɪsˈred/
to read something incorrectly		

Sorry, I've **misread** the label - you only take one tablet before meals.

I thought she likes me, but, I obviously **misread** her signals.

Don't **misread** the instruction; read it thoroughly, step by step.

infinitive	past simple	past participle
mis-set /ˌmɪsˈset/	**mis-set** /ˌmɪsˈset/	**mis-set** /ˌmɪsˈset/
to misplace something, to set something incorrectly		

The apparatus didn't function properly and it turned out that it had been **mis-set**.

Although the worker paid great attention to detail when assembling the devices, he **mis-set** a dozen batches, which then had to be re-assembled.

This model of wristwatch is incredibly complicated and easy to **mis-set**, even by an experienced watchmaker.

infinitive	past simple	past participle
offset /ˈɒfset/	offset /ˈɒfset/	offset /ˈɒfset/
to balance, to compensate for, to emphasise		

He **offset** his lack of protein by eating a steak.

His sharp jawline **offsets** his innate masculinity.

To **offset** work-related stress, she practices yoga and listens to meditation music.

infinitive	past simple	past participle
outbid /ˌaʊtˈbɪd/	outbid /ˌaʊtˈbɪd/	outbid /ˌaʊtˈbɪd/
to make a higher bid, to offer a higher price		

You've been **outbid**. Try to increase your price offer.

We **outbid** all our competitors.

The other company has **outbid** us and won the tender.

infinitive	past simple	past participle
overbid /ˌəʊ.vəˈbɪd/	overbid /ˌəʊ.vəˈbɪd/	overbid /ˌəʊ.vəˈbɪd/
to bid in excess of		

We have been **overbid** by a German company.

I didn't buy it because somebody **overbid** me far in excess of my maximum bid.

Don't even try to **outbid** them - you simply won't have enough money.

infinitive	past simple	past participle
preset /ˌpriːˈset/	preset /ˌpriːˈset/	preset /ˌpriːˈset/
to adjust, to set in advance, to programme		

The focus on this camera is very poor; try to **preset** it before taking photos on location.

I **preset** the washing machine for 3 am so that it would consume less electricity.

I had **preset** my computer to switch itself off but for some reason this didn't happen.

infinitive	past simple	past participle
proofread /ˈpru:fri:d/	proofread /ˈpru:fred/	proofread /ˈpru:fred/
to correct mistakes in text		

The teacher has **proofread** twenty theses so far.

I **proofread** reports for a living.

The manuscript was apparently **proofread** by a professional, but I can still see a lot of mistakes in it.

infinitive	past simple	past participle
put /pʊt/	put /pʊt/	put /pʊt/
to place, to lay, to insert, to suggest, to present, to pose		

He has **put** mutual understanding back a decade with his actions.

I can't remember where I **put** my USB flash drive.

If you **put** it like that, ok, I'll do it.

infinitive	past simple	past participle
quit /kwɪt/	quitted* /ˈkwɪtɪd/ (UK) quit /kwɪt/ (UK) (US)	quitted* /ˈkwɪtɪd/ (UK) quit /kwɪt/ (UK) (US)
to leave, to resign, to stop, to abandon, to give up		

* *according to Collins Dictionary, the past simple and past participle form of the verb **quit** /kwɪt/ is either **quit** /kwɪt/ or **quitted** /ˈkwɪtɪd/. However, the verb **quit** is not commonly used in British English. The past simple or past participle form **quitted**, or more commonly **quit**, if used, tends to be found in literature or very formal texts, especially as a synonym of the verb leave. When talking about an activity which we have stopped doing or given up, the form **quit** is used. On the other hand, the verb **quit** is widely used in American English. However, the past simple and past participle is only **quit**.*

She **quit/quitted** her job without giving notice to her employer.

The firemen told us to **quit** the building immediately as it could collapse at any time.

She **quit/quitted** the apartment after the death of her husband.

infinitive	past simple	past participle
read /ri:d/	read /red/	read /red/
to utter aloud or in one's head the words of a text, to study, to predict		

Have you **read** the article I sent you?

He **read** molecular biology at the University of Melbourne.

The billboard **reads** "Equality for Everybody."

infinitive	past simple	past participle
recast /ˌri:ˈkɑ:st/	recast /ˌri:ˈkɑ:st/	recast /ˌri:ˈkɑ:st/
to cast again, to convert, to change, to adapt		

Although the bell had already been **recast** several times, it maintained its original shape and sound.

The director **recast** all the roles.

The director had a big fight with the male lead and instantly **recast** him with somebody else.

infinitive	past simple	past participle
reset /ˌri:ˈset/	reset /ˌri:ˈset/	reset /ˌri:ˈset/
to set again, to restart		

The doctor has **reset** my broken elbow.

Hold the button for 10 seconds to **reset** the device.

I **reset** the counter by pressing the red button.

infinitive	past simple	past participle
rid /rɪd/	rid /rɪd/	rid /rɪd/
to dispose of, to eliminate, to throw away, to free		

It's hard to **rid** the flat of the smell of garlic.

I **rid** the attic of all its junk.

The whole building was **rid** of hornets that were nesting in the cellar.

infinitive	past simple	past participle
set /set/	set /set/	set /set/
to put, to place, to turn on, to adjust, to arrange, to go down, to decide, to gel		

I've **set** the alarm for 4 am.

They **set** the bench right under the tree, so they could sit and relax there during hot weather.

Have you **set** the date of your birthday banquette?

infinitive	past simple	past participle
shed /ʃed/	shed /ʃed/	shed /ʃed/
to cast off, to give out, to drop, to strew		

The trees had already **shed** their leaves before November.

We **shed** our winter coats and sat next to the fireplace.

I don't like it when my cat **sheds** hair.

infinitive	past simple	past participle
shit /ʃɪt/	shit /ʃɪt/ shat /ʃæt/ shitted /ˈʃɪtɪd/ 🇬🇧	shit /ʃɪt/ shat /ʃæt/ shitted /ˈʃɪtɪd/ 🇬🇧
to poo, to take somebody in		

Note: *the sentences below include vulgar words that some readers might find offensive.*

She's **shit/shat/shitted** in her pants.

Don't go in! Tim **shit/shat/shitted** in the bath and it stinks.

You're **shitting** me! Is that really true?

infinitive	past simple	past participle
shut /ʃʌt/	shut /ʃʌt/	shut /ʃʌt/
to close, to lock		

Shut your mouth!

He **shut** the window and went into the kitchen to make some tea.

That company was **shut** down last year.

infinitive	past simple	past participle
slit /slɪt/	slit /slɪt/	slit /slɪt/
to split, to cut open, to gash		

Use a small knife to **slit** open the envelope.

She **slit** her wrists in an attempt to commit suicide.

The court heard that Brown had **slit** the tires of his ex-girlfriend's car as an act of revenge for leaving him.

infinitive	past simple	past participle
split /splɪt/	split /splɪt/	split /splɪt/
to break up, to snap, to divide		

After the robbery, the gang **split** the stolen money into five piles.

We've just **split** up.

Why do you want to **split** the room in half?

infinitive	past simple	past participle
spread /spred/	spread /spred/	spread /spred/
to stretch, to extend, to coat, to cover, to butter, to get around, to expand, to widen		

If you **spread** the map out, I'll show you where we are.

The plague **spread** at a furious pace.

She **spread** butter liberally on her toast.

infinitive	past simple	past participle
sublet /ˌsʌbˈlet/ sublease /ˌsʌbˈliːs/ 🇺🇸	sublet /ˌsʌbˈlet/ subleased /ˌsʌbˈliːst/ 🇺🇸	sublet /ˌsʌbˈlet/ subleased /ˌsʌbˈliːst/ 🇺🇸
to rent/lease a room, a flat or a house to a subtenant		

I had **sublet** my second flat for five years before I sold it.

I **sublet** my studio flat to my brother three years ago.

If you're not occupying the first floor of your house, you could **sublet** it and earn extra money.

infinitive	past simple	past participle
telecast* /ˈtelikɑːst/	telecast /ˈtelikɑːst/	telecast /ˈtelikɑːst/
to broadcast, to transmit		

****telecast** /ˈtelikɑːst/ is more commonly used in the US. British English speakers would use **broadcast** instead.*

ABC **telecast** the Olympics last year.

The proclamation of President Kennedy was **telecast** live.

We are not planning to **telecast** the next season of this show.

The baseball match was **telecast** at 3 pm while I was still at work.

infinitive	past simple	past participle
thrust /θrʌst/	thrust /θrʌst/	thrust /θrʌst/
to push, to shove, to stab, to jab		

I saw Ryan **thrust** towards me through the crowd.

My boss **thrust** a pile of documents on me and said that he wanted them done by Friday afternoon.

He **thrust** his hands in his pockets, started to whistle and pretended that he was unaware of what was going on.

infinitive	past simple	past participle
typeset /ˈtaɪpset/	typeset /ˈtaɪpset/	typeset /ˈtaɪpset/
to arrange and prepare for printing		

Books are first **typeset,** then printed and bound.

Our publications have already been **typeset** and are ready for printing.

Books that are properly **typeset** give customers a better reading experience.

infinitive	past simple	past participle
underbid /ˌʌndəˈbɪd/	underbid /ˌʌndəˈbɪd/	underbid /ˌʌndəˈbɪd/
to bid less than others		

Our company **underbid** the competition and so won the contract.

With such excellent and skilled professionals, you can **underbid** any rival in the city.

The contractor **underbid** the project but ultimately they couldn't meet our demands.

infinitive	past simple	past participle
undercut /ˌʌndəˈkʌt/	undercut /ˌʌndəˈkʌt/	undercut /ˌʌndəˈkʌt/
to charge less than, to sell cheaply, to undermine		

Our family-owned shop was **undercut** by the big chain store.

Incredibly, they managed to **undercut** their Chinese rivals by 10 %.

Decentralization may have helped my company grow and develop, but at the same time it **undercut** the trust of the managers.

infinitive	past simple	past participle
upset /ʌpˈset/	upset /ʌpˈset/	upset /ʌpˈset/
to worry, to bother, to jog, to jostle, to tip over, to mix up, to overcome, to defeat		

Has he **upset** you?

She **upset** her glass and spilt wine all over the table.

How did you **upset** your opponent?

infinitive	past simple	past participle
wed* /wed/	wed /wed/ wedded /ˈwedɪd/	wed /wed/ wedded /ˈwedɪd/
to get married, to tie the knot		

* *literary/archaic*

Mirabel was only 17 when she **wed/wedded** Prince Randolf, who was nearly 20 years older.

Improbable handsomeness and extraordinary affectionateness were two traits so well **wed/wedded** together in that man that no woman could resist him.

Melanie has always been reticent about her marriage – she was betrothed at sixteen and **wed/wedded** soon after.

infinitive	past simple	past participle
wet /wet/	wet /wet/ wetted /ˈwetɪd/	wet /wet/ wetted /ˈwetɪd/

to soak, to dampen, to water, to moisten

Every morning I **wet** my face with cold water to wake up.

She **wetted/wet** a cloth and put it on his feverish forehead.

He **wetted/wet** his bed.

TESTS

TEST 1

A. Complete the following sentences with the correct past simple form of the verb given in brackets.

1. I initially **(buy)** ____________ his theory but it was later disproven by another scientist.
2. The old hermit **(abide)** ____________ in a cave in the mountains.
3. He **(hang)** ____________ a string of pearls around her neck.
4. He **(speak)** ____________ for two hours but it was worth listening to him.
5. She **(leave)** ____________ her husband after 30 years of marriage.
6. Last summer we **(grow)** ____________ cherry tomatoes in the garden.
7. She **(wear)** ____________ a white dress, which I found inappropriate at a funeral.
8. George **(make)** ____________ a lot of money through writing e-books.
9. Dave **(see)** ____________ his ex-girlfriend yesterday.
10. When the doctor **(unwind)** ____________ the bandage, the injury appeared to have healed.
11. The wind **(swell)** ____________ and began to blow hard.
12. She **(bet)** ____________ me all her wage that I wouldn't do a bungee jump.
13. They **(choose)** ____________ to share a flat and split all the bills.
14. The washing machine **(spin)** ____________ for a few minutes and then broke down.
15. She **(swear)** ____________ loyalty to the company.
16. That faulty electric toaster nearly **(cost)** ____________ me my life.

B. In some of the following sentences the wrong form of the verb in past simple has been used. Correct the sentences which contain an error by crossing out the incorrect form of the verb and writing the correct form next to the sentence. If you think that the sentence does not contain an error, mark the sentence with a tick.

1. Liam had promised his wife to never cheat on her again but **backslidden** after an attractive girl moved in next door. ____________

2. Many contestants on the TV programme **bade** to become the top chef, but there can only ever be one winner. ______________
3. He seemed innocent, but it turned out that it was he who **stole** the money. ______________
4. What I **meant** to tell her was that I love her. ______________
5. He **read** molecular biology at the University of Melbourne. ______________
6. The plane **rised** sharply up into the air. ______________
7. My new jeans **bleeded** during washing and are now very pale. ______________
8. Dewdrops on the grass **shone** in the morning sunlight. ______________
9. She **sung** the song beautifully. ______________
10. She **fed** her employers with lies, every one of which they believed. ______________
11. They **won** the jackpot in the lottery. ______________
12. He **drawed** a caricature of me that was shockingly similar. ______________
13. I didn't have my glasses so couldn't see what the clock actually **said.** ______________
14. My eyes **stang** after I got soap in them while washing my face. ______________
15. It **took** us almost a month to refurbish the house after the flood. ______________
16. The prisoner **strucked** a prison officer before being wrestled to the ground. ______________

TEST 2

A. Complete the following sentences with the correct past simple form of the verb given in brackets.

1. I **(think)** ____________ you wouldn't take the joke so seriously.
2. Not even the best specialists knew where his unusual health condition **(arise)** ____________ from.
3. The gangster boss already **(bestride)** ____________ the entire district and nothing would stop him from taking over the whole city.

4. She **(fling)** ____________ her bag in the corner and sat down with a strong drink.
5. She has **(tear)** ____________ her dress on a fence.
6. He forgot to set up the alarm and **(oversleep)** ____________.
7. Commitment and hard work **(underlie)** ____________ his success.
8. My brother-in-law **(sell)** ____________ me on the idea that portfolio investment was profitable.
9. The phone **(ring)** ____________ several times, but no one was there when I picked up.
10. I have **(get)** ____________ better at speaking English since I started a course.
11. Judge Moore **(uphold)** ____________ the lower court's decision.
12. Legend has it that St George **(slay)** ____________ the dragon.
13. The queen was **(clothe)** ____________ in fine silks.
14. I can't remember where I **(put)** ____________ my USB flash drive.
15. My landlord refused to repair the fridge and I **(bear)** ____________ the cost of the repairs myself.
16. The children **(swing)** ____________ on a rope over the river.
17. These two tribes not only live at peace, but they are also strongly **(bind)** ____________ together by the same rituals and beliefs.
18. Josh **(outgrow)** ____________ his older brother a few months ago and is now a centimetre taller.

B. In some of the following sentences the wrong form of the verb in past simple has been used. Correct the sentences which contain an error by crossing out the incorrect form of the verb and writing the correct form next to the sentence. If you think that the sentence does not contain an error, mark the sentence with a tick.

1. The children **diged** a long tunnel in the snow. ______________
2. Tragically, he **lost** both parents soon after he was born. ______________
3. It was you who **gave** me the flu. ______________
4. They **faught** bravely but were eventually overrun by the enemy. ______________
5. The room had no air-conditioning and we **sweated** all night. ______________
6. The farmer **sewed** the sunflower seeds in several rows. ______________

7. A bizarre creature **wove** between the trees and vanished without trace. ______________
8. Mike used to be the Chief Financial Officer (CFO) and so always **oversaw** the budget. ______________
9. I **found** my old photos in the attic. ______________
10. He almost **weept** with joy when she announced that she was expecting his child. ______________
11. The problems **laid** in our lack of mutual understanding. ______________
12. The old lady **broke** her leg after slipping on the kitchen floor. ______________
13. Beethoven **wrote** nine complete symphonies. ______________
14. She **relayed** the carpet in the bedroom because it needed some adjustment. ______________
15. That old comedy really **slew** me. ______________
16. The castle **sat** on a high mountain. ______________
17. He blindly **clang** to the hope that she would return. ______________
18. A little boy **stuck** his tongue out to me. ______________

TEST 3

A. Complete the following sentences with the correct past participle form of the verb given in brackets.

1. A flock of wild geese has just **(fly)** ____________ over our house.
2. Nobody knows how the pyramids of Giza were actually **(build)** ________.
3. I don't like my steak **(overdo)** ____________.
4. Don't make her angry, she has just **(wake)** ____________ up.
5. He has **(grind)** ____________ so many cigarette butts into the table that it's now permanently scarred.
6. His latest diary entry has **(bespeak)** ____________ his true eloquence in the art of journaling.
7. Oliver had **(deal)** ____________ in cars for a living before setting up his own restaurant.
8. Why haven't you **(lay)** ____________ the table yet?

9. The Lady of Shalott's heart was **(rive)** ____________ with distress when her mirror cracked.
10. She has **(undertake)** ____________ to arrange all formalities for the trip to China.
11. Being fired has **(teach)** ____________ me a valuable life lesson: don't argue with your boss.
12. The director has definitely **(miscast)** ____________ the lead role, but no one can convince him otherwise.
13. I don't think Luiza has ever quite **(forgive)** ____________ her husband for cheating on her.
14. I've **(beseech)** ____________ him three times not to leave us.
15. Sorry I'm late, but I was **(waylay)** ____________ by the boss.
16. The edges of this fabric must be **(sew)** ____________ with black thread.
17. Sorry, I've **(misread)** ____________ the label - you only take one tablet before meals.
18. The whole building was **(rid)** ____________ of hornets that were nesting in the cellar.

B. In some of the following sentences the wrong form of the verb in past participle has been used. Correct the sentences which contain an error by crossing out the incorrect form of the verb and writing the correct form next to the sentence. If you think that the sentence does not contain an error, mark the sentence with a tick.

1. All production has been **hamstringed** by lack of labour. ____________
2. He'd **cost** the entire investment and decided that it was unprofitable. ____________
3. Josh has **blown** all his money and now wants to borrow some from me. ____________
4. Heavy rainfall has been **forecasted** for today on the East Coast. ____________
5. The flat had **stank** of fried fish until they opened the windows. ____________
6. She has **knitted** this pattern many times before. ____________
7. "The Lord of the Rings" trilogy was **shooted** entirely in New Zealand. ____________
8. About 80% of the tuition fees were **born** by my university. ____________

9. We have been **overbid** by a German company. ______________

10. He has **bend** so often to pick up litter that he now has a permanent stoop. ______________

11. I have **felt** the same way all along. ______________

12. Our team was **beaten** by only 1 point. ______________

13. Have you **readden** a horse before? ______________

14. Her response has completely **threwn** me. I now don't know what to do. ______________

15. Her behaviour has **led** me to believe that she can be trusted. ______________

16. That statue had **standed** for centuries before it was destroyed. ______________

17. He hasn't **mowed** the lawn yet. ______________

18. His works have **withstanded** the test of time. ______________

TEST 4

A. Complete the following sentences with the correct past participle form of the verb given in brackets.

1. I was **(chide)** ____________ for being rude to my teacher.
2. Your words have **(hurt)** ____________ her deeply. You need to apologise.
3. We've just **(begin)** ____________ to celebrate our 10th wedding anniversary.
4. We haven't been **(give)** ____________ permission to do that.
5. I've already **(show)** ____________ you how the machine works, haven't I?
6. I've **(wind)** ____________ (up) my watch but it still won't work.
7. We've just **(catch)** ____________ the last train to London.
8. You should have **(seek)** ____________ legal advice before you took any action.
9. I'd completely **(forget)** ____________ about the meeting.
10. I'm sure he didn't say that. You must have **(mishear)** ____________ him.
11. The new water park has **(bring)** ____________ many families to our city.
12. These two subplots in the book are skilfully **(interweave)** ____________.

13. We've **(send)** ____________ you all the details.
14. He has **(for(e)go)** ____________ holidays abroad in order to save up for a house.
15. You're **(mistake)** ____________ - he had nothing to do with it.
16. He's **(sleep)** ____________ only two hours.

B. In some of the following sentences the wrong form of the verb in past participle has been used. Correct the sentences which contain an error by crossing out the incorrect form of the verb and writing the correct form next to the sentence. If you think that the sentence does not contain an error, mark the sentence with a tick.

1. His salary was **withhold** after they suspected him of embezzlement. ____________
2. Alec has **outdroven** everybody else – and it was the furthest shot in his golfing career. ____________
3. After the storm I saw that a massive tree had **fallen** less than a metre away from my car. ____________
4. The barber has **shorned** my hair and trimmed my beard. ____________
5. They've been **driven** by a desire to maximise profit. ____________
6. She has **ran** away from home and we're trying to find her. ____________
7. It is too early to celebrate our success and that is why I have **forbore** giving any further details on this matter. ____________
8. America has **withdrawn** its troops from Iraq. ____________
9. Have you **paid** the electricity bill this month? ____________
10. Maria has **resit** the French examination twice but still failed to pass. ____________
11. He's **drank** too much beer. ____________
12. We think they've been deliberately **mislead**. ____________
13. The trees had already **sheded** their leaves before November. ____________
14. I'm sorry, but all the buns are **gone**. ____________
15. Brad has **forsworn** the criminal life he has been leading for many years. ____________
16. She has **proved** her innocence and has been set free. ____________

TEST 5

A. Complete the following sentences with the correct past simple or past participle form of the verb given in brackets.

1. I've **(do)** ____________ a few French lessons now, but can still only order a cup of tea!
2. After Peter's third denial of Jesus, the rooster **(crow)** ____________ a second time.
3. She **(relay)** ____________ the news to everybody as soon as she returned home.
4. Diane **(awake)** ____________ at the crack of dawn.
5. If he hadn't **(overtake)** ____________ the other car, he wouldn't have caused the accident.
6. He **(hang)** ____________ himself.
7. I've **(saw)** ____________ several boards.
8. She **(inlay)** ____________ rubies into the earrings.
9. Where **(be)** ____________ you last Saturday?
10. He **(burst)** ____________ into laughter and couldn't say a word.
11. I told him to buy a gluten-free cake, but he **(misunderstand)** ____________ and bought a sugar-free cake.
12. The main square was **(strew)** ____________ with litter after the concert.
13. The bone of his broken wrist **(knit)** ____________ together very quickly.
14. Where have you **(hide)** ____________ the children's Christmas gifts?
15. I had **(sublet)** ____________ my second flat for five years before I sold it.
16. The exam **(overrun)** ____________ by 30 minutes.

B. In some of the following sentences the wrong form of the verb in past simple or past participle has been used. Correct the sentences which contain an error by crossing out the incorrect form of the verb and writing the correct form next to the sentence. If you think that the sentence does not contain an error, mark the sentence with a tick.

1. She **kneeled** for the whole Mass. ______________
2. I've just **swam** 40 lengths of the pool and feel shattered. ______________

3. Although I **held** the umbrella tightly in my hand, the wind managed to whip it away. ____________
4. The mafia had **wrunged** a huge amount of protection money out of the owner of the casino. ____________
5. Elizabeth was tall and slender, so any long dress **became** her. ____________
6. My boss **thrust** a pile of documents on me and said that he wanted them done by Friday afternoon. ____________
7. I've **heared** that you've got engaged. Congratulations! ____________
8. She **wound** the baby after feeding it to make it easier to burp. ____________
9. She was **forbade** from meeting her friends. ____________
10. The Bible says that Adam **begot** Cain and Abel. ____________
11. The lake is **rung** with tall evergreen conifers. ____________
12. My phone screen **froze** and I couldn't press any buttons. ____________
13. The tide was so strong that it **sweeped** the yacht out to sea. ____________
14. How long have you **known** each other? ____________
15. After the Second World War, the map of Europe was **redrew**. ____________
16. She **slang** her coat on a peg and went to the living room. ____________

TEST 6

A. Complete the following sentences with the correct past simple or past participle form of the verb given in brackets.

1. She has **(weave)** ____________ many replica tapestries for refurbished castles.
2. She **(wet)** ____________ a cloth and put it on his feverish forehead.
3. I was **(browbeat)** ____________ into signing the contract.
4. They've **(have)** ____________ a lot of difficulties in their marriage.
5. We **(rewind)** ____________ the tape to replay a passage about the man who robs the local shops.

6. Though the walls of his mansion appear to be **(bestrew)** ____________ with some of the world's most famous paintings, many, in fact, are simply copies.
7. He **(tell)** ____________ them not to buy him any presents for his birthday this year.
8. All the tests we've carried out are invalid and will have to be **(retake)** ____________.
9. Either rats or mice **(bite)** _____________ the cables and caused a short-circuit in the whole building.
10. She **(upset)** ____________ her glass and spilled wine all over the table.
11. Nevertheless, it's true. It doesn't matter that I **(overhear)** __________ him.
12. She has **(tear)** ____________ her dress on a fence.
13. In recent months she has **(undergo)** ____________ many changes in her professional and private life.
14. She **(strive)** ____________ to please everyone, not understanding that it wasn't the way to get everyone to like her.
15. The Queen has **(partake)** __________ in many interesting events this year.
16. Residents were **(shake)** ____________ to hear of the murder in their street.

B. In some of the following sentences the wrong form of the verb in past simple or past participle has been used. Correct the sentences which contain an error by crossing out the incorrect form of the verb and writing the correct form next to the sentence. If you think that the sentence does not contain an error, mark the sentence with a tick.

1. The doctor told me that, despite the treatment, the tumour hadn't **shrunked** any further. ______________
2. Simon **came** to help me out last week. ______________
3. Mirabel was only 17 when she **wed** Prince Randolf, who was nearly 20 years older. ______________
4. Diana **kepted** a diary nearly all her life. ______________
5. Guilt over causing a colleague's death **ate** into him every day. ______________
6. Turning around, I **beholded** a tall woman dressed in black staring at me with a murderous look. ______________
7. The ferry **sank** in the middle of the river. ______________
8. He must have **creapt** in when I wasn't looking. ______________

9. The police **bid** everyone to evacuate the building immediately. ______________
10. The court heard that Brown had **slited** the tires of his ex-girlfriend's car as an act of revenge for leaving him. ______________
11. The boys **slinked** out of the house and went to the park. ______________
12. She has **laid** to everyone. ______________
13. She **understood** from the nuns that life in the convent would make her a better person. ______________
14. I had **meet** him before, but couldn't remember his name. ______________
15. A drunk driver has **sped** down the road and crashed into a lamppost. ______________
16. My family have **broke** with tradition and decided to have goose instead of turkey this Christmas. ______________

TEST 7

A. The following sentences contain forms of the verb in past simple and past participle used mainly in British English. Write next to the sentence the past simple or past participle forms of the verb used mainly or also in American English.

1. Her dress **shrank** when she washed it in hot water. ______________
2. Dennis **knelt** down on one knee and proposed to Dorothy. ______________
3. Oh, no! Look what I've **trodden/trod** in! ______________
4. The high jumper **outleapt** all competitors to claim a gold medal. ______________
5. She lay down on the grass and **daydreamt**. ______________
6. My cat **leapt** up on the windowsill to look at the birds in the garden. ______________
7. We've just had solar panels **fitted** to the roof of the house. ______________
8. She has **proved** her innocence and has been set free. ______________
9. The cake **smelt** really good and tasted even better. ______________
10. My cat **sprang** from my arms onto the floor. ______________

11. I have **got** better at speaking English since I started a course. ____________
12. Many English words were **spelt** differently in the past. ____________
13. The entire building **burnt** to the ground in the fire. ____________
14. She's just **spilt** coffee on my new carpet! ____________
15. Don't make her angry, she has just **woken** up. ____________
16. The spider has **span** a web. ____________

B. The following sentences contain the past simple and past participle forms of the verb preferred mainly in American English. Write next to the sentence the past simple or past participle forms of the verb used mainly or also in British English.

1. Petrol has **gotten** so expensive recently. ____________
2. He **learned** Spanish when he lived in Barcelona. ____________
3. He **spit** the food out because it tasted horrible. ____________
4. Without any doubt, the concert **stunk**. ____________
5. He had **pled** innocent to the crime but the judge found him guilty. ____________
6. The performance was **broadcasted** live all over Europe. ____________
7. My orchids have **thriven** since I placed them in indirect sunlight. ____________
8. You have **misspelled** my second name. ____________
9. I've **sawed** several boards. ____________
10. He **dwelled** by a lake for twenty years. ____________
11. Sharron completely **spoiled** my birthday party by getting drunk. ____________
12. The submersible **dove** to a depth of 10,000 feet. ____________
13. He sank to his knees, **rended** his garments and yelled hopelessly in a language that nobody could understand. ____________
14. The cat **snuck** up on the mouse and pounced on it. ____________
15. The pine **leaned** over under the weight of the snow. ____________
16. He has **dreamed** of being an astronaut since he was 8. ____________

TABLE OF IRREGULAR VERBS

infinitive	past simple	past participle
abide /əˈbaɪd/	abode [1,4] /əˈbəʊd/ abided /əˈbaɪdɪd/	abode [1,4] /əˈbəʊd/ abided /əˈbaɪdɪd/
alight /əˈlaɪt/	alighted /əˈlaɪtɪd/ alit [5] /əˈlɪt/	alighted /əˈlaɪtɪd/ alit [5] /əˈlɪt/
arise /əˈraɪz/	arose /əˈrəʊz/	arisen /əˈrɪzən/
awake /əˈweɪk/	awoke /əˈwəʊk/	awoken /əˈwəʊ.kən/
backslide /ˈbæk.slaɪd/	backslid /ˈbæk.slɪd/	backslid /ˈbæk.slɪd/ backslidden /ˈbæk.slɪdᵊn/
be /biː/	was /wɒz/ were /wɜːr/	been /biːn/
bear /beər/	bore /bɔːr/	born [1] /bɔːn/ borne /bɔːn/
beat /biːt/	beat /biːt/	beaten /ˈbiː.tən/
become /bɪˈkʌm/	became /bɪˈkeɪm/	become /bɪˈkʌm/
beget /bɪˈget/	begot /bɪˈgɒt/ begat [1] /bɪˈgæt/	begot /bɪˈgɒt/ begotten [1] /bɪˈgɒtᵊn/
begin /bɪˈgɪn/	began /bɪˈgæn/	begun /bɪˈgʌn/
behold [2,3] /bɪˈhəʊld/	beheld /bɪˈheld/	beheld /bɪˈheld/
bend /bend/	bent /bent/	bent /bent/
beseech [2] /bɪˈsiːtʃ/	beseeched /bɪˈsiːtʃəd/ besought /bɪˈsɔːt/	beseeched /bɪˈsiːtʃəd/ besought /bɪˈsɔːt/
beset [4] /bɪˈset/	beset /bɪˈset/	beset /bɪˈset/
bespeak /bɪˈspiːk/	bespoke /bɪˈspəʊk/	bespoken /bɪˈspəʊkən/
bestrew [2] /bɪˈstruː/	bestrewed /bɪˈstruːd/	bestrewed /bɪˈstruːd/ bestrewn /bɪˈ struːn/
bestride [4]/bɪˈstraɪd/	bestrode /bɪˈstrəʊd/	bestridden /bɪˈstrɪdn/
bet /bet/	bet /bet/	bet /bet/
bid /bɪd/	bid /bɪd/	bid /bɪd/

infinitive	past simple	past participle
bid [1,2] /bɪd/	bade /bæd/, /beɪd/ bid /bɪd/	bidden /ˈbɪdᵊn/ bid /bɪd/
bind /baɪnd/	bound /baʊnd/	bound /baʊnd/
bite /baɪt/	bit /bɪt/	bitten /ˈbɪt.ən/
bleed /bli:d/	bled /bled/	bled /bled/
blow /bləʊ/	blew /blu:/	blown /bləʊn/
break /breɪk/	broke /brəʊk/	broken /ˈbrəʊ.kən/
breed /bri:d/	bred /bred/	bred /bred/
bring /brɪŋ/	brought /brɔ:t/	brought /brɔ:t/
broadcast /ˈbrɔ:dkɑ:st/	broadcast /ˈbrɔ:dkɑ:st/ broadcasted /ˈbrɔ:dkɑ:stɪd/	broadcast /ˈbrɔ:dkɑ:st/ broadcasted /ˈbrɔ:dkɑ:stɪd/
browbeat /ˈbraʊ.bi:t/	browbeat /ˈbraʊ.bi:t/	browbeaten /ˈbraʊbi:tᵊn/
build /bɪld/	built /bɪlt/	built /bɪlt/
burn /bɜ:n/	burnt /bɜ:nt/ burned /bɜ:nd/	burnt /bɜ:nt/ burned /bɜ:nd/
burst /bɜ:st/	burst /bɜ:st/	burst /bɜ:st/
bust /bʌst/	bust /bʌst/ busted /ˈbʌstɪd/	bust /bʌst/ busted /ˈbʌstɪd/
buy /baɪ/	bought /bɔ:t/	bought /bɔ:t/
can /kæn/, /kən/	could /kʊd/, /kəd/	could /kʊd/, /kəd/
cast /kɑ:st/	cast /kɑ:st/	cast /kɑ:st/
catch /kætʃ/	caught /kɔ:t/	caught /kɔ:t/
chide /tʃaɪd/	chided /tʃaɪdɪd/ chid [5] /tʃɪd/	chided /tʃaɪdɪd/ chid [5] /tʃɪd/ chidden [5] /ˈtʃɪdᵊn/
choose /tʃu:z/	chose /tʃəʊz/	chosen /ˈtʃəʊ.zən/
cleave /kli:v/	cleaved /kli:vd/ cleft [1]/klɛft/	cleaved /kli:vd/ cleft [1]/klɛft/

infinitive	past simple	past participle
	clove /kləʊv/	cloven [1]/kləʊvn/
cling /klɪŋ/	clung /klʌŋ/	clung /klʌŋ/
clothe /kləʊð/	clad /klæd/ clothed /kləʊðd/	clad /klæd/ clothed /kləʊðd/
come /kʌm/	came /keɪm/	come /kʌm/
cost /kɒst/	cost /kɒst/ costed [1] /ˈkɒstɪd/	cost /kɒst/ costed [1] /ˈkɒstɪd/
creep /kriːp/	crept /krept/	crept /krept/
crossbreed /ˈkrɒs.briːd/	crossbred /ˈkrɒs.bred/	crossbred /ˈkrɒs.bred/
crow /krəʊ/	crowed /krəʊd/ crew [5] /kruː/	crowed /krəʊd/
cut /kʌt/	cut /kʌt/	cut /kʌt/
daydream /ˈdeɪ.driːm/	daydreamt /ˈdeɪ.dremt/ daydreamed /ˈdeɪ.driːmd/	daydreamt /ˈdeɪ.dremt/ daydreamed /ˈdeɪ.driːmd/
deal /diːl/	dealt /delt/	dealt /delt/
dig /dɪg/	dug /dʌg/	dug /dʌg/
dive /daɪv/	dived /daɪvd/ dove /doʊv/	dived /daɪvd/
do /duː/	did /dɪd/	done /dʌn/
draw /drɔː/	drew /druː/	drawn /drɔːn/
dream /driːm/	dreamt /dremt/ dreamed /driːmd/	dreamt /dremt/ dreamed /driːmd/
drink /drɪŋk/	drank /dræŋk/	drunk /drʌŋk/
drive /draɪv/	drove /drəʊv/	driven /ˈdrɪv.ən/
dwell [2, 4] /dwel/	dwelt /dwelt/ dwelled /dweld/	dwelt /dwelt/ dwelled /dweld/
eat /iːt/	ate /et/, /eɪt/	eaten /ˈiːtᵊn/
fall /fɔːl/	fell /fel/	fallen /ˈfɔː.lən/

infinitive	past simple	past participle
feed /fi:d/	fed /fed/	fed /fed/
feel /fi:l/	felt /felt/	felt /felt/
fight /faɪt/	fought /fɔ:t/	fought /fɔ:t/
find /faɪnd/	found /faʊnd/	found /faʊnd/
fit /fɪt/	fitted /ˈfɪtɪd/ 🇬🇧 fit /fɪt/ 🇺🇸	fitted /ˈfɪtɪd/ 🇬🇧 fit /fɪt/ 🇺🇸
flee /fli:/	fled /fled/	fled /fled/
fling /flɪŋ/	flung /flʌŋ/	flung /flʌŋ/
fly /flaɪ/	flew /flu:/	flown /fləʊn/
forbear [4] /fɔ:ˈbeər/	forbore /fɔ:ˈbɔ:r/	forborne /fɔ:ˈbɔ:n/
forbid /fəˈbɪd/	forbade /fəˈbæd/, /fəˈbeɪd/	forbidden /fəˈbɪd.ən/
forecast /ˈfɔ:kɑ:st/	forecast /ˈfɔ:kɑ:st/ forecasted /ˈfɔ:kɑ:stɪd/	forecast /ˈfɔ:kɑ:st/ forecasted /ˈfɔ:kɑ:stɪd/
forego/forgo [4] /fɔ:ˈgəʊ/	forewent /fɔ:ˈwɛnt/ forwent /fɔ:ˈwɛnt/	foregone /ˌfɔ:.gɒn/ forgone /ˌfɔ:.gɒn/
foresee /fəˈsi:/	foresaw /fɔ:ˈsɔ:/	foreseen /fɔ:ˈsi:n/
foretell /fɔ:ˈtel/	foretold /fɔ:ˈtəʊld/	foretold /fɔ:ˈtəʊld/
forget /fəˈget/	forgot /fəˈgɒt/	forgotten /fəˈgɒtn/
forgive /fəˈgɪv/	forgave /fəˈgeɪv/	forgiven /fəˈgɪvn/
forsake [2] /fəˈseɪk/	forsook /fəˈsʊk/	forsaken /fəˈseɪkən/
forswear [2, 4] /fɔ:ˈsweər/	forswore /fɔ:ˈswɔ:/	forsworn /fɔ:ˈswɔ:n/
freeze /fri:z/	froze /frəʊz/	frozen /ˈfrəʊzən/
get /get/	got /gɒt/	got /gɒt/ gotten [1]/ˈgɒt.ən/ 🇺🇸
gild [2] /gɪld/	gilded /gɪldɪd/ gilt /gɪlt/	gilded /gɪldɪd/ gilt /gɪlt/
give /gɪv/	gave /geɪv/	given /gɪvn/
go /gəʊ/	went /went/	gone /gɒn/

infinitive	past simple	past participle
grind /graɪnd/	ground /graʊnd/	ground /graʊnd/
grow /grəʊ/	grew /gruː/	grown /grəʊn/
hamstring /ˈhæmstrɪŋ/	hamstrung /ˈhæmstrʌŋ/	hamstrung /ˈhæmstrʌŋ/
handwrite /ˈhændraɪt/	handwrote /ˈhændrəʊt/	handwritten /ˈhændrɪtn/
hang /hæŋ/	hung /hʌŋ/ hanged [1] /hæŋd/	hung /hʌŋ/ hanged [1] /hæŋd/
have /hæv/, /həv/	had /hæd/,/həd/	had /hæd/,/həd/
hear /hɪər/	heard /hɜːd/	heard /hɜːd/
hew /hjuː/	hewed /hjuːd/	hewed /hjuːd/ hewn /hjuːn/
hide /haɪd/	hid /hɪd/	hidden /hɪdn/
hit /hɪt/	hit /hɪt/	hit /hɪt/
hold /həʊld/	held /held/	held /held/
hurt /hɜːt/	hurt /hɜːt/	hurt /hɜːt/
inlay /ˌɪnˈleɪ/	inlaid /ˌɪnˈleɪd/	inlaid /ˌɪnˈleɪd/
input /ˈɪnpʊt/	input /ˈɪnpʊt/ inputted /ˈɪnpʊtɪd/	input /ˈɪnpʊt/ inputted /ˈɪnpʊtɪd/
interweave /ˌɪn.təˈwiːv/	interwove /ˌɪn.təˈwəʊv/	interwoven/ˌɪn.təˈwəʊvən/
keep /kiːp/	kept /kept/	kept /kept/
kneel /niːl/	knelt /nelt/ kneeled /niːld/	knelt /nelt/ kneeled /niːld/
knit /nɪt/	knit [1] /nɪt/ knitted /ˈnɪtɪd/	knit [1] /nɪt/ knitted /ˈnɪtɪd/
know /nəʊ/	knew /njuː/	known /nəʊn/
lade [3] /leɪd/	laded /leɪdɪd/	laden /ˈleɪd^{ə}n/ laded /leɪdɪd/
lay /leɪ/	laid /leɪd/	laid /leɪd/
lead /liːd/	led /led/	led /led/
lean /liːn/	leant /lent/	leant /lent/

infinitive	past simple	past participle
	leaned /liːnd/	leaned /liːnd/
leap /liːp/	leapt /lept/ leaped /liːpt/	leapt /lept/ leaped /liːpt/
learn /lɜːn/	learnt /lɜːnt/ learned /lɜːnd/	learnt /lɜːnt/ learned /lɜːnd/
leave /liːv/	left /left/	left /left/
lend /lend/	lent /lent/	lent /lent/
let /let/	let /let/	let /let/
lie /laɪ/	lay /leɪ/ lied [1] /laɪd/	lain /leɪn/ lied [1] /laɪd/
light /laɪt/	lit /lɪt/ lighted [1] /ˈlaɪ.tɪd/	lit /lɪt/ lighted [1] /ˈlaɪ.tɪd/
lip-read /ˈlɪp riːd/	lip-read /ˈlɪp red/	lip-read /ˈlɪp red/
lose /luːz/	lost /lɒst/	lost /lɒst/
make /meɪk/	made /meɪd/	made /meɪd/
mean /miːn/	meant /ment/	meant /ment/
meet /miːt/	met /met/	met /met/
miscast /ˌmɪsˈkɑːst/	miscast /ˌmɪsˈkɑːst/	miscast /ˌmɪsˈkɑːst/
misdeal /ˌmɪsˈdiːl/	misdealt /ˌmɪsˈdelt/	misdealt /ˌmɪsˈdelt/
mishear /ˌmɪsˈhɪər/	misheard /ˌmɪsˈhɜːd/	misheard /ˌmɪsˈhɜːd/
mishit /ˌmɪsˈhɪt/	mishit /ˌmɪsˈhɪt/	mishit /ˌmɪsˈhɪt/
mislay [4] /ˌmɪsˈleɪ/	mislaid /ˌmɪsˈleɪd/	mislaid /ˌmɪsˈleɪd/
mislead /ˌmɪsˈliːd/	misled /mɪs’led/	misled /mɪs’led/
misread /ˌmɪsˈriːd/	misread /ˌmɪsˈred/	misread /ˌmɪsˈred/
misset /ˌmɪsˈset/	misset /ˌmɪsˈset/	misset /ˌmɪsˈset/
misspeak /ˌmɪsˈspiːk/	misspoke /ˌmɪsˈspəʊk/	misspoken /ˌmɪsˈspəʊkn/
misspell /ˌmɪsˈspel/	misspelt /ˌmɪsˈspelt/ misspelled /ˌmɪsˈspeld/	misspelt /ˌmɪsˈspelt/ misspelled /ˌmɪsˈspeld/

infinitive	past simple	past participle
misspend /ˌmɪsˈspend/	misspent /ˌmɪsˈspent/	misspent /ˌmɪsˈspent/
mistake /mɪˈsteɪk/	mistook /mɪˈstʊk/	mistaken /mɪˈsteɪkən/
misunderstand /ˌmɪs.ʌn.dəˈstænd/	misunderstood /mɪsʌndəˈstʊd/	misunderstood /mɪsʌndəˈstʊd/
mow /məʊ/	mowed /məʊd/	mown /məʊn/ mowed /məʊd/
offset /ˈɒfset/	offset /ˈɒfset/	offset /ˈɒfset/
outbid /ˌaʊtˈbɪd/	outbid /ˌaʊtˈbɪd/	outbid /ˌaʊtˈbɪd/
outdo /ˌaʊtˈduː/	outdid /ˌaʊtˈdɪd/	outdone /ˌaʊtˈdʌn/
outdrink /ˌaʊtˈdrɪŋk/	outdrank /ˌaʊtˈdræŋk/	outdrunk /ˌaʊtˈdrʌŋk/
outdrive /ˌaʊtˈdraɪv/	outdrove /ˌaʊtˈdrəʊv/	outdriven /ˌaʊtˈdrɪvᵊn/
outfight /ˌaʊtˈfaɪt/	outfought /ˌaʊtˈ/fɔːt /	outfought /ˌaʊtˈ/fɔːt /
outgrow /ˌaʊtˈgrəʊ/	outgrew /ˌaʊtˈgruː/	outgrown /ˌaʊtˈgrəʊn/
outleap /ˈaʊt.liːp/	outleapt /ˈaʊt.liːpt/ 🇬🇧 outleaped /ˈaʊt.liːpt/ 🇺🇸	outleapt /ˈaʊt.liːpt/ 🇬🇧 outleaped /ˈaʊt.liːpt/ 🇺🇸
outsell /ˌaʊtˈsel/	outsold /ˌaʊtˈsəʊld/	outsold /ˌaʊtˈsəʊld/
outshine /ˌaʊtˈʃaɪn/	outshone /ˌaʊtˈʃɒn /	outshone /ˌaʊtˈʃɒn /
overbid /ˌəʊ.vəˈbɪd/	overbid /ˌəʊ.vəˈbɪd/	overbid /ˌəʊ.vəˈbɪd/
overcome /ˌəʊ.vəˈkʌm/	overcame /ˌəʊ.vəˈkeɪm/	overcome /ˌəʊ.vəˈkʌm/
overdo /ˌəʊ.vəˈduː/	overdid /ˌəʊ.vəˈdɪd/	overdone /ˌəʊ.vəˈdʌn/
overdraw /ˌəʊ.vəˈdrɔː/	overdrew /ˌəʊvəˈdruː/	overdrawn /ˌəʊvəˈdrɔːn/
overeat /əʊ.vəˈiːt/	overate /əʊ.vəˈet/ /əʊ.vəˈeɪt/	overeaten /əʊ.vəˈiːtn/
overfeed /ˌəʊvəˈfiːd/	overfed /ˌəʊvəˈfed/	overfed /ˌəʊvəˈfed/
overfly /əʊ.vəˈflaɪ/	overflew /əʊ.vəˈfluː/	overflown /əʊ.vəˈfləʊn/
overhang /ˌəʊ.vəˈhæŋ/	overhung /ˌəʊ.vəˈhʌŋ/	overhung /ˌəʊ.vəˈhʌŋ/
overhear /ˌəʊ.vəˈhɪər/	overheard /ˌəʊ.vəˈhɜːd/	overheard /ˌəʊ.vəˈhɜːd/
overlay /ˌəʊ.vəˈleɪ/	overlaid /ˌəʊ.vəˈleɪd/	overlaid /ˌəʊ.vəˈleɪd/

infinitive	past simple	past participle
overpay /ˌəʊ.və'peɪ/	overpaid /ˌəʊ.və'peɪd/	overpaid /ˌəʊ.və'peɪd/
override /əʊ.və'raɪd/	overrode /əʊ.və'rəʊd/	overridden /əʊ.və'rɪdn/
overrun /ˌəʊ.və'rʌn/	overran /ˌəʊ.və'ræn/	overrun /ˌəʊ.və'rʌn/
oversee /ˌəʊ.və'si:/	oversaw /ˌəʊ.və'sɔ: /	overseen /ˌəʊ.və' si:n /
oversell /ˌəʊ.və'sel/	oversold /ˌəʊ.və'sold/	oversold /ˌəʊ.və'sold/
overshoot /ˌəʊ.və'ʃu:t/	overshot /ˌəʊ.və'ʃɒt /	overshot /ˌəʊ.və'ʃɒt /
oversleep /ˌəʊ.və'sli:p/	overslept /ˌəʊ.və'slept/	overslept /ˌəʊ.və'slept/
overspend/ˌəʊ.və'spend/	overspent /ˌəʊ.və'spent/	overspent /ˌəʊ.və'spent/
overtake /ˌəʊvə'teɪk/	overtook /ˌəʊvə'tʊk /	overtaken /ˌəʊvə'teɪkən/
overthrow /ˌəʊvə'θrəʊ/	overthrew /ˌəʊvə'θru:/	overthrown /ˌəʊ.və'θrəʊn /
partake [3, 4] /pɑ:'teɪk/	partook /pɑ:'tʊk/	partaken /pɑ:'teɪkən/
pay /peɪ/	paid /peɪd/	paid /peɪd/
plead /pli:d/	pleaded /pli:dɪd/ pled /pled/	pleaded /pli:dɪd/ pled /pled/
prepay /ˌpri:'peɪ/	prepaid /ˌpri:'peɪd/	prepaid /ˌpri:'peɪd/
preset /ˌpri:'set/	preset /ˌpri:'set/	preset /ˌpri:'set/
proofread /'pru:fri:d/	proofread /'pru:fred/	proofread /'pru:fred/
prove /pru:v/	proved /pru:vd/	proved /pru:vd/ proven /pru:vn/
put /pʊt/	put /pʊt/	put /pʊt/
quit /kwɪt/	quitted /'kwɪtɪd/ quit /kwɪt/	quitted /'kwɪtɪd/ quit /kwɪt/
read /ri:d/	read /red/	read /red/
rebuild /ˌri:'bɪld/	rebuilt /ˌri:'bɪlt/	rebuilt /ˌri:'bɪlt/
recast /ˌri:'kɑ:st/	recast /ˌri:'kɑ:st/	recast /ˌri:'kɑ:st/
redo /ri:'du:/	redid /ri:'dɪd /	redone /ri:'dʌn /
redraw /ˌri:'drɔ:/	redrew /ˌri:'dru:/	redrawn /ˌri:'drɔ:n /

infinitive	past simple	past participle
relay /ˌrɪˈleɪ/	relaid /ˌrɪˈleɪd/ relayed [1] /ˌrɪˈleɪd/	relaid /ˌrɪˈleɪd/ relayed [1] /ˌrɪˈleɪd/
remake /ˌriːˈmeɪk/	remade /ˌriːˈmeɪd/	remade /ˌriːˈmeɪd/
rend [2, 3] /rend/	rent /rent/ rended /rendɪd/	rent /rent/ rended /rendɪd/
repay /rɪˈpeɪ/	repaid /rɪˈpeɪd/	repaid /rɪˈpeɪd/
rerun /ˌriːˈrʌn/	reran /ˌriːˈræn/	rerun /ˌriːˈrʌn/
resell /ˌriːˈsel/	resold /ˌriːˈsəʊld/	resold /ˌriːˈsəʊld/
reset /ˌriːˈset/	reset /ˌriːˈset/	reset /ˌriːˈset/
resit /ˌriːˈsɪt/	resat /ˌriːˈsæt/	resat /ˌriːˈsæt/
retake /ˌriːˈteɪk/	retook /ˌriːˈtʊk /	retaken /ˌriːˈteɪkən /
retell /ˌriːˈtel/	retold /ˌriːˈtəʊld /	retold /ˌriːˈtəʊld /
rethink /ˌriːˈθɪŋk/	rethought /ˌriːˈθɔːt/	rethought /ˌriːˈθɔːt/
rewind /ˌriːˈwaɪnd/	rewound /ˌriːˈwaʊnd/	rewound /ˌriːˈwaʊnd/
rewrite /ˌriːˈraɪt/	rewrote /ˌriːˈrəʊt /	rewritten /ˌriːˈrɪtn /
rid /rɪd/	rid /rɪd/	rid /rɪd/
ride /raɪd/	rode /rəʊd/	ridden /rɪdn/
ring /rɪŋ/	rang /ræŋ/ ringed [1] /rɪŋd/	rung /raŋ/ ringed [1] /rɪŋd/
rise /raɪz/	rose /rəʊz/	risen /rɪzn/
rive [2, 3] /raɪv/	rived /raɪvd/	riven /ˈrɪvᵊn/ rived /raɪvd/
run /rʌn/	ran /ræn/	run /rʌn/
saw /sɔː/	sawed /sɔːd/	sawn /sɔːn/ sawed /sɔːd/
say /seɪ/	said /sed/	said /sed/
see /siː/	saw /sɔː/	seen /siːn/
seek [4] /siːk/	sought /sɔːt/	sought /sɔːt/

infinitive	past simple	past participle
sell /sel/	sold /səʊld/	sold /səʊld/
send /send/	sent /sent/	sent /sent/
set /set/	set /set/	set /set/
sew /səʊ/	sewed /səʊd/	sewed /səʊd/ sewn /səʊn/
shake /ʃeɪk/	shook /ʃʊk/	shaken /ˈʃeɪkən/
shear /ʃɪər/	sheared /ʃɪəd/	sheared /ʃɪəd/ shorn /ʃɔːn/
shed /ʃed/	shed /ʃed/	shed /ʃed/
shine /ʃaɪn/	shone /ʃɒn/	shone /ʃɒn/
shit [7] /ʃɪt/	shit /ʃɪt/ shat /ʃæt/ shitted /ˈʃɪtɪd/	shit /ʃɪt/ shat /ʃæt/ shitted /ˈʃɪtɪd/
shoe /ʃuː/	shod /ʃɒd/	shod /ʃɒd/
shoot /ʃuːt/	shot /ʃɒt/	shot /ʃɒt/
show /ʃəʊ/	showed /ʃəʊd/	shown /ʃəʊn/ showed [5] /ʃəʊd/
shrink /ʃrɪŋk/	shrank /ʃræŋk/ shrunk /ʃrʌŋk/	shrunk /ʃrʌŋk/
shrive [3] /ʃraɪv/	shrove /ʃrəʊv/	shriven /ˈʃrɪvᵊn/
shut /ʃʌt/	shut /ʃʌt/	shut /ʃʌt/
sing /siŋ/	sang /sæŋ/	sung /saŋ/
sink /sɪŋk/	sank /sæŋk/	sunk /saŋk/
sit /sɪt/	sat /sæt/	sat /sæt/
sky-write /skaɪ’raɪt /	sky-wrote /skaɪ’rəʊt /	sky-written /skaɪˈrɪt.ən /
slay [2, 3] /sleɪ/	slew /sluː/ slayed [1] /sleɪd/	slain /sleɪn/ slayed [1] /sleɪd/
sleep /sliːp/	slept /slept/	slept /slept/
slide /slaɪd/	slid /slɪd/	slid /slɪd/

infinitive	past simple	past participle
sling /slɪŋ/	slung /slʌŋ/	slung /slʌŋ/
slink /slɪŋk/	slunk /slʌŋk/	slunk /slʌŋk/
slit /slɪt/	slit /slɪt/	slit /slɪt/
smell /smel/	smelt /smelt/ 🇬🇧 smelled /smeld/ 🇺🇸 🇬🇧	smelt /smelt/ 🇬🇧 smelled /smeld/ 🇺🇸 🇬🇧
smite [2, 3] /smaɪt/	smote /sməʊt/	smitten /ˈsmɪtᵊn/
sneak /sniːk/	sneaked /sniːkt/ snuck [6] /snʌk/ 🇺🇸	sneaked /sniːkt/ snuck [6] /snʌk/ 🇺🇸
sow /səʊ/	sowed /səʊd/	sown /səʊn/ sowed /səʊd/
speak /spiːk/	spoke /spəʊk/	spoken /ˈspəʊ.kən/
speed /spiːd/	speeded /ˈspiːdɪd/ sped /sped/	speeded /ˈspiːdɪd/ sped /sped/
spell /spel/	spelt /spelt/ 🇬🇧 spelled /speld/ 🇺🇸 🇬🇧	spelt /spelt/ 🇬🇧 spelled /speld/ 🇺🇸 🇬🇧
spend /spend/	spent /spent/	spent /spent/
spill /spɪl/	spilt /spɪlt/ 🇬🇧 spilled /spɪld/ 🇺🇸 🇬🇧	spilt /spɪlt/ 🇬🇧 spilled /spɪld/ 🇺🇸 🇬🇧
spin /spɪn/	spun /spʌn/	spun /spʌn/ span /spæn/ 🇬🇧
spit /spɪt/	spat /spæt/ spit /spɪt/ 🇺🇸	spat /spæt/ spit /spɪt/ 🇺🇸
split /splɪt/	split /splɪt/	split /splɪt/
spoil /spɔɪl/	spoilt /spɔɪlt/ 🇬🇧 spoiled /spɔɪld/ 🇬🇧 🇺🇸	spoilt /spɔɪlt/ 🇬🇧 spoiled /spɔɪld/ 🇬🇧 🇺🇸
spread /spred/	spread /spred/	spread /spred/
spring /sprɪŋ/	sprang /spræŋ/ 🇬🇧 🇺🇸 sprung /sprʌŋ/ 🇺🇸	sprung /sprʌŋ/
stand /stænd/	stood /stʊd/	stood /stʊd/
steal /stiːl/	stole /stəʊl/	stolen /ˈstəʊlən/

infinitive	past simple	past participle
stick /stɪk/	stuck /stʌk/	stuck /stʌk/
sting /stɪŋ/	stung /stʌŋ/	stung /stʌŋ/
stink /stɪŋk/	stank /stæŋk/ stunk /stʌŋk/	stunk /stʌŋk/
strew /stru:/	strewed /stru:d/	strewn /stru:n/ strewed /stru:d/
stride /straɪd/	strode /strəʊd/	stridden /ˈstridən/
strike /straɪk/	struck /strʌk/	struck /strʌk/
string /strɪŋ/	strung /strʌŋ/	strung /strʌŋ/
strive [4] /straɪv/	strove /strəʊv/ strived /straɪvd/	striven /ˈstrɪvn/ strived /straɪvd/
sublet /ˌsʌbˈlet/ sublease /ˌsʌbˈli:s/	sublet /ˌsʌbˈlet/ subleased /ˌsʌbˈli:st/	sublet /ˌsʌbˈlet/ subleased /ˌsʌbˈli:st/
swear /sweə/	swore /swɔ:/	sworn /swɔ:n/
sweat /swet/	sweated /ˈswetɪd/ sweat [1] /swet/	sweated /ˈswetɪd/ sweat [1] /swet/
sweep /swi:p/	swept /swept/	swept /swept/
swell /swel/	swelled /sweld/	swollen /ˈswəʊlən/
swim /swɪm/	swam /swæm/	swum /swʌm/
swing /swɪŋ/	swung /swʌŋ/	swung /swʌŋ/
take /teɪk/	took /tʊk/	taken /ˈteɪkən/
teach /ti:tʃ/	taught /tɔ:t/	taught /tɔ:t/
tear /tɛə/	tore /tɔ:/	torn /tɔ:n/
telecast /ˈtelikɑ:st/	telecast /ˈtelikɑ:st/	telecast /ˈtelikɑ:st/
tell /tel/	told /təʊld/	told /təʊld/
think /θɪŋk/	thought /θɔ:t/	thought /θɔ:t/
thrive /θraɪv/	thrived /θraɪvd/ throve [5] /θrəʊv/	thrived /θraɪvd/ thriven [5] /ˈθrɪvᵊn/
throw /θrəʊ/	threw /θru:/	thrown /θrəʊn/

infinitive	past simple	past participle
thrust /θrʌst/	thrust /θrʌst/	thrust /θrʌst/
tread /tred/	trod /trɒd/ treaded /tredid/	trodden /trɒdn/ trod /trɒd/ treaded /tredid/
typeset /ˈtaɪpset/	typeset /ˈtaɪpset/	typeset /ˈtaɪpset/
unbend /ˌʌnˈbend/	unbent /ˌʌnˈbent/	unbent /ˌʌnˈbent/
unbind /ʌnˈbaɪnd/	unbound /ʌnˈbaʊn.d/	unbound /ʌnˈbaʊn.d/
underbid /ˌʌndəˈbɪd/	underbid /ˌʌndəˈbɪd/	underbid /ˌʌndəˈbɪd/
undercut /ˌʌndəˈkʌt/	undercut /ˌʌndəˈkʌt/	undercut /ˌʌndəˈkʌt/
undergo /ˌʌn.dəˈgəʊ/	underwent /ˌʌn.dəˈwent /	undergone /ˌʌn.dəˈ gɒn /
underlie [4] /ˌʌn.dəˈlaɪ/	underlay /ˌʌndərˈleɪ /	underlain /ˌʌndəˈleɪn/
underpay /ˌʌndəˈpeɪ/	underpaid /ˌʌndəˈpeɪd/	underpaid /ˌʌndəˈpeɪd/
undersell /ˌʌndəˈsel/	undersold /ˌʌndəˈsəʊld/	undersold /ˌʌndəˈsəʊld/
understand/ˌʌndəˈstænd/	understood /ˌʌndəˈstʊd/	understood /ˌʌndəˈstʊd/
undertake /ˌʌndəˈteɪk/	undertook /ˌʌndəˈtʊk/	undertaken /ˌʌndəˈteɪkən/
underwrite /ˌʌn.dərˈaɪt/	underwrote /ˌʌn.dərˈrəʊt /	underwritten/ˌʌn.dərˈrɪt.ən /
undo /ʌnˈdu:/	undid /ʌnˈdɪd/	undone /ʌnˈdʌn/
unfreeze /ʌnˈfri:z/	unfroze /ʌnˈfrəʊz/	unfrozen /ʌnˈfrəʊzn/
unmake /ʌnˈmeɪk/	unmade /ʌnˈmeɪd/	unmade /ʌnˈmeɪd/
unsay /ʌnˈseɪ/	unsaid /ʌnˈsed/	unsaid /ʌnˈsed/
unwind /ˌʌnˈwaɪnd/	unwound /ˌʌnˈwaʊnd/	unwound /ˌʌnˈwaʊnd/
uphold /ʌpˈhəʊld/	upheld /ʌpˈheld/	upheld /ʌpˈheld/
upset /ʌpˈset/	upset /ʌpˈset/	upset /ʌpˈset/
wake /weɪk/	woke /wəʊk/ waked /weɪkd/	woken /ˈwəʊ.kən/ waked /weɪkd/
waylay /weɪˈleɪ/	waylaid /weɪˈleɪd/	waylaid /weɪˈleɪd/
wear /weə/	wore /wɔ:/	worn /wɔ:n/

infinitive	past simple	past participle
weave /wi:v/	wove /wəʊv/ weaved [1] /wi:vd/	woven /ˈwəʊvən/ weaved [1] /wi:vd/
wed /wed/	wed /wed/ wedded /ˈwedɪd/	wed /wed/ wedded /ˈwedɪd/
weep /wi:p/	wept /wept/	wept /wept/
wet /wet/	wet /wet/ wetted /ˈwetɪd/	wet /wet/ wetted /ˈwetɪd/
win /wɪn/	won /wʌn/	won /wʌn/
wind /waɪnd/ wind [1] /wɪnd/	wound /waʊnd/ winded [1] /wɪndɪd/	wound /waʊnd/ winded [1] /wɪndɪd/
withdraw /wɪðˈdrɔ:/	withdrew /wɪðˈdru:/	withdrawn /wɪðˈdrɔ:n/
withhold [4] /wɪðˈhəʊld/	withheld /wɪðˈheld/	withheld /wɪðˈheld/
withstand [4] /wɪðˈstænd/	withstood /wɪðˈstʊd/	withstood /wɪðˈstʊd/
wring /rɪŋ/	wrung /rʌŋ/	wrung /rʌŋ/
write /raɪt/	wrote /rəʊt/	written /rɪtn/

[1] form of a verb used in a different sense or used in specific circumstances
[2] form of a verb used literary
[3] form of a verb considered archaic
[4] form of a verb used in formal language
[5] form of a verb used very rarely
[6] form of a verb used in spoken language
[7] taboo

ANSWER KEY

QUIZ 1

1. a
2. b
3. c
4. b
5. a
6. b
7. a, c

QUIZ 2

1. b
2. b
3. a
4. c
5. a, d
6. a
7. a

QUIZ 3

1. b
2. a, c
3. a, c
4. b
5. a
6. c

QUIZ 4

1. b
2. a
3. c
4. a
5. b, c
6. b

QUIZ 5

1. b
2. c
3. c
4. b
5. a
6. a

QUIZ 6

1. a, b
2. c
3. b
4. played
5. smiled
6. b

QUIZ 7

1. b
2. a

3. b
4. c
5. b
6. a

TEST 1

A

1. bought
2. abided or abode
3. hung
4. spoke
5. left
6. grew
7. wore
8. made
9. saw
10. unwound
11. swelled
12. bet
13. chose
14. spun
15. swore
16. cost

B

1. backslid
2. bid
3. ✓
4. ✓
5. read
6. rose
7. bled
8. ✓
9. sang
10. ✓
11. ✓
12. drew
13. ✓
14. stung
15. ✓
16. struck

TEST 2

A

1. thought
2. arose
3. bestrode
4. flung
5. torn
6. overslept

B

1. dug
2. ✓
3. ✓
4. fought
5. sweat
6. sowed

7. underlay
8. sold
9. rang
10. got
11. upheld
12. slew
13. clothed
14. put
15. bore
16. swung
17. bound
18. outgrew

7. weaved
8. ✔
9. ✔
10. wept
11. lay
12. ✔
13. ✔
14. relaid
15. slayed
16. sat
17. clung
18. ✔

TEST 3

A

1. flown
2. built
3. overdone
4. woken
5. ground
6. bespoken
7. dealt
8. laid
9. riven *or* rived
10. undertaken
11. taught
12. miscast
13. forgiven
14. beseeched *or* besought
15. waylaid
16. sewn *or* sewed
17. misread
18. rid

B

1. hamstrung
2. costed
3. ✔
4. ✔ forecast *or* forecasted
5. stunk
6. ✔ knitted *or* knit
7. shot
8. borne
9. ✔
10. bent
11. ✔
12. ✔
13. ridden
14. thrown
15. ✔
16. stood
17. ✔ mowed *or* mown
18. withstood

TEST 4

	A		B
1.	chided	1.	withheld
2.	hurt	2.	outdriven
3.	begun	3.	✔
4.	given	4.	sheared *or* shorn
5.	shown	5.	✔
6.	wound	6.	run
7.	caught	7.	forborne
8.	sought	8.	✔
9.	forgotten	9.	✔
10.	misheard	10.	resat
11.	brought	11.	drunk
12.	interwoven	12.	misled
13.	sent	13.	shed
14.	forgone *also* foregone	14.	✔
15.	mistaken	15.	forsworn
16.	slept	16.	✔

TEST 5

	A		B
1.	done	1.	✔ knelt *or* kneeled
2.	crowed *or rarely* crew	2.	swum
3.	relayed	3.	✔
4.	awoke	4.	wrung
5.	overtaken	5.	✔
6.	hanged	6.	✔
7.	sawn	7.	heard
8.	inlaid	8.	winded
9.	were	9.	forbidden
10.	burst	10.	begat

11. misunderstood
12. strewn *or* strewed
13. knit
14. hidden
15. sublet
16. overran

11. ringed
12. ✔
13. swept
14. ✔
15. redrawn
16. slung

TEST 6

A

1. woven
2. wet *or* wetted
3. browbeaten
4. had
5. rewound
6. bestrewed *or* bestrewn
7. told
8. retaken
9. bit
10. upset
11. overheard
12. torn
13. undergone
14. strove *or* strived
15. partaken
16. shaken

B

1. shrunk
2. ✔
3. ✔ wed *or* wedded
4. kept
5. ✔
6. beheld
7. ✔
8. crept
9. ✔ bade *or* bid
10. slit
11. slunk
12. lied
13. ✔
14. met
15. ✔
16. broken

TEST 7

A 🇺🇸

1. shrunk
2. kneeled
3. treaded
4. outleaped

B 🇬🇧

1. got
2. learnt
3. spat
4. stank

5. daydreamed
6. leaped
7. fit
8. proven
9. smelled
10. sprung
11. gotten
12. spelled
13. burned
14. spilled
15. waked
16. spun

5. pleaded
6. broadcast
7. thrived
8. misspelt
9. sawn
10. dwelt
11. spoilt
12. dived
13. rent
14. sneaked
15. leant
16. dreamt

INDEX

A

B

C

D

E

F

G

H

I

K

L

M

O

P

Q

R

S

T

U

W

NOTES

NOTES

NOTES

Printed by Amazon Italia Logistica S.r.l.
Torrazza Piemonte (TO), Italy